Ry $3.07

W9-DJN-202

AMERICAN AUTHORS AND CRITICS SERIES

Published by Barnes & Noble under the general editorship of FOSTER PROVOST and JOHN MAHONEY of Duquesne University and with the sponsorship of that university.

ABOUT THE AUTHOR

FRANK BALDANZA is Assistant Professor in the English Department of Bowling Green State University and has taught at Georgia Institute of Technology and Louisiana State University. Professor Baldanza has contributed many articles to leading professional journals.

Samuel L. Clemens

MARK TWAIN

An Introduction and Interpretation

FRANK BALDANZA

BOWLING GREEN STATE UNIVERSITY

Barnes & Noble, Inc.   New York

Publishers   Booksellers   Since 1873

To HARPER & BROTHERS appreciation is expressed for permission to quote from the works of Mark Twain, including the following: *Mark Twain's Autobiography*, edited by A. B. Paine; *Mark Twain in Eruption*, edited by Bernard DeVoto; *The Mysterious Stranger;* and *What Is Man?* Also, for permission to quote from *Mark Twain's Letters*, edited by A. B. Paine; *Mark Twain: A Biography*, by A. B. Paine; *My Father: Mark Twain*, by Clara Clemens; and *My Mark Twain*, by W. D. Howells.

Permission from the publisher to reprint from the following is gratefully acknowledged: Henry Nash Smith and William M. Gibson, *Mark Twain-Howells Letters: The Correspondence of Samuel L. Clemens and William Dean Howells 1872–1910*, The Belknap Press of Harvard University Press, Copyright, 1960 by the Mark Twain Company, Mildred Howells, and John Mead Howells, and the President and Fellows of Harvard College. To the same publisher acknowledgment is made for permission to quote from *Mark Twain at Work*, by Bernard DeVoto.

Acknowledgment is made to the Public Trustee and the Society of Authors for permission to quote from the *Plays of Bernard Shaw;* to George Fields Publisher for permission to quote from *The Washoe Giant in San Francisco;* and to the Viking Press for permission to quote from *The Portable Mark Twain*.

This book is an original work (No. 3) in the American Authors & Critics Series. It was written by a distinguished educator, carefully edited, and produced in accordance with the highest standards of publishing. The text was set on the Linotype in Old Style No. 7 by Plimpton Press (Norwood, Mass.). The paper for this edition was manufactured by the S. D. Warren Company (Boston, Mass.) and supplied by the Canfield Paper Company (New York, N.Y.). This edition was printed by the Plimpton Press (Norwood, Mass.) and bound by Sendor Bindery (New York, N.Y.). The cover was designed by Rod Lopez-Fabrega.

PREFACE

THIS STUDY of the life and works of Mark Twain is intended for both the general reader and the student. The aim has been to provide a succinct and thorough survey of his life that takes into account all the biographical research that has been done since A. B. Paine's monumental authorized biography.

The chapters on Twain's works are meant as a general introduction for the non-specialist, with some attention to his technique as a humorist. These chapters have been organized in a unique manner, treating the autobiographical, the travel, the historical, the juvenile, the American, and the polemical writings as units in themselves. This grouping draws attention away from the somewhat specious attempt to discover measured chronological growth in a writer whose productions were often sporadic and spontaneous, and it concentrates on fresh insights to be drawn from the inter-relations of the works themselves.

I am grateful to Dr. Morris Golden for invaluable criticism of the manuscript, and to Bowling Green State University for a research grant that enabled me to complete my work. I wish to thank Drs. Foster Provost and John Mahoney and Mr. Elbert Epler of Barnes & Noble for genial editorial assistance.

CONTENTS

ILLUSTRATIONS

CHRONOLOGY

1835 Samuel Langhorne Clemens born November 30, in Florida, Missouri.

1839 Moved with family to Hannibal, Missouri.

1847 Began work as a printer's apprentice after death of his father in March.

1853–4 Left Hannibal for printing work in St. Louis, New York, and Philadelphia where he was correspondent for the Muscatine, Iowa *Journal*.

1855–7 Worked as printer in Keokuk, Iowa, and Cincinnati.

1857–60 Pilot on the Mississippi.

1861 Departed in July with brother Orion for Nevada. Following year spent prospecting for silver.

1862–4 Reporter on *Virginia City Territorial Enterprise*.

1864 Reporter for San Francisco *Morning Call* (May–December).

1864–5 Returned to prospecting.

1866 March–August, traveled to Sandwich Islands (Hawaii). In October, delivered his first lecture. Set out for New York in December.

1867 June–November, made *Quaker City* voyage to Europe and the Holy Land as correspondent for the San Francisco *Alta California*.

1869 Bought a third interest in the Buffalo *Express*.

1870 Married Olivia Langdon in February.

1870 Birth of son, Langdon.

1871 Sold interest in *Express*. Family moved to Hartford, Connecticut in October.

1872 Birth of daughter, Susan, in March. Death of Langdon in June. August–November, traveled to England. *Roughing It* published.

1873 Trip to England. Published *The Gilded Age*.

1874 Birth of daughter, Clara, in June.

1876 Published *The Adventures of Tom Sawyer*.

1878–9   Made trip to Europe.

1880   Daughter, Jean, born in July. Published *A Tramp Abroad*.

1882   *The Prince and the Pauper* published.

1883   *Life on the Mississippi* published.

1884–5   Made lecture tour with George W. Cable.

1885   *Adventures of Huckleberry Finn* published.

1889   *A Connecticut Yankee in King Arthur's Court* published.

1891–5   Lived in Europe.

1894   *Pudd'nhead Wilson* published.

1895   August to July, 1896, made round-the-world lecture tour.

1896   Death of Susan in August. Continued residence in Europe until 1900. *Joan of Arc* published.

1897   *Following the Equator* published.

1901   Received honorary degree from Yale University.

1902   Received honorary degree from the University of Missouri.

1903–4   Lived in Florence, Italy.

1904   Mrs. Clemens died in June.

1907   Received honorary degree from Oxford University.

1908   Clemens moved to Stormfield, Redding, Connecticut.

1909   Death of Jean in December.

1910   Death of Samuel Langhorne Clemens in April.

1962   Death of Clara in November.

1

❦ THE MAN

DURING his life, Samuel Langhorne Clemens enjoyed an international fame that has probably never been equalled by any
other American author. Beleaguered by autograph hunters and
private correspondents, invited incessantly to every imaginable
kind of social observance, honored by Yale and Oxford, cheered by
dockhands, haunted by reporters, begged for advice on all subjects,
he came to see himself as a sort of informal ambassador to the
world. With Benjamin Franklin and Abraham Lincoln, two other
famous Americans to whom he is occasionally compared, he shared
peculiar characteristics. Like the former, he pursued an immense
range of disparate interests, and like the latter, he developed his
final vocation (as a "literary person") relatively late in life. As he
was about to begin his duties as a newspaper editor in Buffalo in
1869, he looked back over his first thirty-four years as "a foolish
life *made up* of apprenticeships." [1] These included early careers
as printer, steamboat pilot, soldier, miner, journalist and lecturer—
and even after finding his metier as a writer, he became involved
in ruinous financial experiments as a publisher and as a manu-
facturer of typesetting machines.

Throughout his life, he maintained an engaging and infectiously
boyish enthusiasm that led his wife to nickname him "Youth." Un-

[1] Dixon Wecter, ed., *Mark Twain to Mrs. Fairbanks* (San Marino, California, Huntington Library, 1949), p. 103.

I

like most men, Samuel Clemens never did renounce his boyhood; he carried with him into maturity miraculously preserved and vibrant memories of his early and middle adolescence, and it was through these memories that he filtered his adult experience. At the age of fifty-five he wrote to an unknown correspondent: "And yet I can't go away from the boyhood period & write novels because *capital* [that is, personal experience] is not sufficient by itself & I lack the other essential: interest in handling the men & experiences of later times." [2] On this circumstance he founded an enviable fame and fortune and an enduring artistic achievement.

❦

Clemens was born in Florida, Missouri, in November of 1835. He struggled for health during his early years; but as he conquered constitutional weaknesses, he developed a troublesome cussedness that distinguished him as a child from his elder and younger brothers, Orion and Henry. His mischievousness led to a series of escapades: several times nearly drowning, purposefully contracting measles, smoking, rolling rocks down a hill before church-bound carriages, and running away from home. He early exhibited the first signs of his lifelong nervous sensibility in his sleepwalking and exaggerated guilt feelings. These characteristics were augmented by the impression made on him by Calvinist Sunday School doctrines and the fearful superstitions of Negro slaves that were part of his Missouri boyhood.

As a child in the towns of Florida and Hannibal, Missouri, Sam spent idyllic summers on the farm of his Uncle, John Quarles, and was involved in the peccadillos of the "gang" as immortalized in *Tom Sawyer* and *Huckleberry Finn*. But there were disturbing experiences, too: the young boy saw slave beatings, a murder, and corpses. One biographer even argues that Sam accidentally witnessed a post-mortem on his father's body. His successful beginning as a printer's apprentice at the age of eleven led him from work on Orion's Hannibal *Journal* to St. Louis, New York, and Philadelphia, before he returned to his brother's printing establishment in Keokuk, Iowa. Then the fever for exotic areas and rapid wealth infected him with a sudden enthusiasm for commercial exploitation of the Amazon; this, the first of his spectacular fiascos, led accidentally to an apprenticeship under the colorful

2 Bernard DeVoto, ed., *The Portable Mark Twain* (New York, The Viking Press, 1946), p. 9. Brackets DeVoto's.

Horace Bixby as a pilot on the Mississippi River. Along with his boyhood memories, this experience was to provide some of the richest ore for his great books. A comic-opera interlude as a constantly retreating Confederate soldier soured him on military service. Then the equivocal nature of his "retirement" from army life made him uncomfortable enough to go West with Orion, newly appointed as Secretary to the Territory of Nevada.

He took to silver mining with a buoyant enthusiasm, reveling in dreams of sudden and immense wealth; in the end, however, the gruelling punishment of the primitive living conditions and the drain on his savings from his piloting career took their toll. It was almost with a sense of surrender that he finally presented himself in August, 1862, at the office of the *Virginia City Territorial Enterprise*, unkempt and dirty after a long trek, to accept a $25.00 a week job as reporter. Here he repeated the kind of success he had had as a printer and pilot, quickly gaining a reputation as journalistic hoaxer and parliamentary reporter for the Territorial Legislature.

In the free atmosphere of Nevada journalism he slowly refined his comic technique, although he manifested a peculiar talent for misjudging the occasion and the audience. At least one of the factors in his leaving Nevada in 1864 was the local furor caused by his assertion that the Carson City ladies meant to contribute funds collected for a Civil War sanitation fund to a miscegenation society. He found a berth with the San Francisco *Morning Call,* and he took with him his now immortal pseudonym, Mark Twain, a leadsman's call indicating that the ship is in a safe two fathoms. On this newspaper (although the strictness of its policy cramped him) he began a life-long preoccupation with humane causes, championing the underdog and the defeated, as his mother had always done in Hannibal: in San Francisco he stood up for the harried Chinese immigrant; later he fulminated against the condition of an unkempt cemetery in Buffalo, the overcharging of his servants by taxi-drivers, vivisection, Tammany corruption, exploitation of natives in the Congo, the bondage of Russian serfs, the limitations of the copyright, and the like. But he was not consistent in his reforming zeal: later in his life he refused to publish material attacking coal monopolies or Standard Oil out of loyalty to his father-in-law, a coal magnate, and H. H. Rogers, a Standard Oil executive friend.

He hated the weary drudgery of decorous big-city journalism, and when a brawl between a close friend and a bartender who

3

had special police connections brought him into conflict with a powerful city machine in San Francisco, he rather hastily retired to mining again. In the meantime, acquaintanceship with Artemus Ward and Bret Harte had given him a concept of literary vocation that made this miner a different person from the earlier one. It was during this sojourn in Calaveras County that "the wild humorist of the Pacific slope" heard in an Angel Camp tavern the celebrated jumping frog tale that was to be the beginning of his Eastern fame.

In 1866 the Sacramento *Union* sent him on a trip to Hawaii (then called the Sandwich Islands). This initiated the role as travel correspondent that was to take him periodically to Europe, and later on a world cruise. At this time, he also began lecturing, an outgrowth of his governorship of a burlesque Legislature held by Nevada newspapermen and lawmakers. Although he grew to dislike the travel and what he felt to be the cheapening effort of the performance, he continued to resort to lecturing when pressed for money, sometimes bringing in as much as $1,600 in a single night.

The following year he sailed on the *Quaker City* for an extended tour of Europe and the Holy Land, on a voyage sponsored by the San Francisco *Daily Alta California*. He wrote travel letters for this journal as well as for the New York *Tribune* and *Herald*. As yet, he had no intention of becoming an author; in a letter to his mother and sister, he says "But I had my mind made up to *one* thing—I wasn't going to touch a book unless there was *money* in it, and a good deal of it." [3] When he did revise the newspaper letters into *The Innocents Abroad,* his first successful book, this monetary aim was richly satisfied.

The most notable personal experience of the European voyage had occurred one day when the boat was anchored in the Bay of Smyrna. A fellow passenger, Charles Langdon, had shown Clemens an ivory miniature of his formerly invalid sister Olivia. Clemens, who was apparently deeply impressed by her beauty, met Olivia during the holidays of 1867–8 in New York, when he attended a Dickens reading with her, her brother, and her father. All the enthusiasm that her picture had inspired was justified. Clemens fascinated her father, Jervis Langdon, and gradually became more and more welcome as a guest at their home in Elmira, New York. His attentions to Olivia, however, were very coolly

[3] Albert Bigelow Paine, ed., *Mark Twain's Letters* (New York, Harper and Brothers, 1911). p. 145.

received; and it was not until early in 1869 that he finally gained her consent and the family's. The marriage took place one year later. In the meantime, he worked briefly in Washington as secretary to Senator Stewart of Nevada. His love for Olivia, and his intense need for her, as revealed in his love letters, is at the same time heartily moving and a bit pathetic. The force of the emotion is impressive, but the helpless surrender and boy-like worship also exhibited there reveal a tenderness that cries out for motherly solicitude.

He continued, meanwhile, his successes as a lecturer and newspaper correspondent, and *The Innocents Abroad* was selling extremely well. Since the book had received a good review in the *Atlantic Monthly*, Clemens stopped by the office in Boston to thank the editor, William Dean Howells. This meeting initiated one of the closest and most sustained literary friendships on record. The two writers corresponded for the rest of their lives, visiting back and forth whenever possible. Although their collaboration on a play was unsuccessful, they did manage to publish a collection of American humor. Aside from these frenzied and relatively unsuccessful projects, Howells rendered Clemens an immense service by reading proof for all of his major books, by advising Clemens about prolixity, vulgarity, and lapses of tone, and by publishing favorable reviews. In return, Clemens praised Howells' books privately, but rendered sparse literary aid to his friend. In fact, Clemens was frequently reprimanded by Howells (partly in jest, certainly) for not reading enough of his work. Aside from their correspondence, Howells' *My Mark Twain* is the most enthusiastic and the most judicious appreciation of Clemens' highest qualities as a writer and as a man.

Six months before his marriage, Clemens bought (on a loan from his father-in-law) a third interest in the Buffalo *Express*. For this journal and in a "Memoranda" column of the New York *Galaxy*, he chose to write items of humorous and sentimental interest, continuing from time to time in the outraged emotions of the reformer. He wrote a series of satiric letters based on Goldsmith, in which a Chinese immigrant describes the inhumanity with which he is treated in America. He also attacked a New York minister who refused to bury a famous actor, thus popularizing the "Little Church Around the Corner," which *did* perform the service. His stands on national affairs revealed him as a Republican, having become thoroughly "de-Southernized," in Howells' phrase.

But plagued by the distractions of illness and death in the

family, and the nursing of their first and premature baby, Langdon, Clemens ceased writing for the *Galaxy* and sold his interest in the *Express* (at a loss) in April, 1871. The family moved from the luxurious wedding-gift home that had been totally furnished for them by the Langdons to Quarry Farm, near Elmira, an idyllic retreat owned by his wife's sister and her husband. Here Clemens was later to compose some of his greatest work in the now-famous octagonal study.

In the fall, they moved to Hartford, Connecticut, where Clemens had already been a frequent visitor and where the circle of literati, including Charles Dudley Warner and Harriet Beecher Stowe, promised congenial times. He continued lecturing, and early in 1872 published *Roughing It,* largely an account of his days in the West and in Hawaii.

That summer, the death of his son Langdon engulfed him in the familiar guilt fantasies that plagued his life. These had begun with the death of his father, whom he felt he had failed. They were strongly intensified on the death of his brother Henry in the explosion of the steamboat *Pennsylvania* in 1858, for which Clemens held himself personally accountable. Shortly before Henry left New Orleans, he and Sam discussed how they would behave in case of an accident, and Sam felt that his advice had caused Henry to return to the boat to help survivors. As a result Henry accidentally inhaled steam and suffered a lingering and painful death. Secondly, as he nursed his brother, he insisted that an untrained assistant administer morphine, which he later assumed to be a contributing factor in the death. He also claimed to have had a premonitory dream, exact in every detail, of Henry's funeral. Moreover, in Langdon's case, he said he had contributed to the infant's death by inadvertently exposing him to cold during a carriage ride. While it is impossible to ascertain the specific degree of Clemens' guilt, it is clear that his hypersensitivity combined with his Presbyterian Sunday School training to torture the man unduly.

In spite of these problems, in 1872 he made his first triumphal trip to England, a country that he always regarded with warm feeling. On his return, he collaborated with his Hartford neighbor, Charles Dudley Warner, on his first novel, *The Gilded Age,* published in 1873. Another trip to England, this time including an unprecedentedly successful lecture series, was followed on his return to America by "Old Times on the Mississippi" in the *Atlantic Monthly* in 1875 and *Tom Sawyer* in 1876. In the meantime, in 1874, he built a princely mansion in Nook Farm, an exclusive, "literary" area of Hartford. Regardless of his foreign honors and widespread fame at home, the icy reception given by some Boston newspapers to his Whittier birthday speech late in 1877 (in which three drunken Western tramps impersonate Longfellow, Emerson, and Holmes) again intensified his feelings of insecurity despite the forgiveness of the principals involved. He and his family sailed for an extended stay in Germany, afterward traveling through Switzerland, Italy, and France—experiences recorded in *A Tramp Abroad* (1880)—and returning in the fall of 1879. There followed the publication of *The Prince and the Pauper* in 1882, and a trip to his old haunts on the Mississippi in order to expand the *Atlantic* articles into *Life on the Mississippi* (1883).

The first of his great financial imbroglios began in his establishment of the Charles L. Webster publishing company, managed by his nephew. Webster had already directed Clemens' expensive adventure in kaolatype, a chalk engraving process, that cost $40,-000 to $50,000 before its abandonment; but in the nephew's hands *Huckleberry Finn* (1885) sold well, and the great *coup* was the memoirs of General Grant, produced laboriously and feverishly as the author died of cancer. The first royalty check which Clemens paid the widow ($200,000) was the largest single payment in the history of publishing at that time. Clemens had been nurtured on his own father's magniloquent speeches about the riches to be realized from the family tract of Tennessee land, and he appears to have learned nothing from his father's failures. He was weaned on the wild dreams (and sometimes wilder reality) of mining speculation. It is little wonder, then, that he should have intoxicated himself with illusions of financial glory. What is surprising is the way at least the Grant memoirs justified the vision, because succeeding books including the supposedly great bonanza of an authorized life of Pope Leo XIII, barely paid for themselves.

Coupled with this gambling fever was the abiding fascination with inventions, gadgets, and fads already exhibited in the kaolatype experiment. He invented self-adjusting vest-straps, and was interested in patented grape scissors, a steam generator, a steam pulley, and marine telegraphy. He claimed to be the first person to use a typewriter for literary purposes, and the first to run a telephone wire to a private home. He predicted long-distance telephoning. He was among the first persons to use the fountain pen, the accordion letter file, the early high-wheeled bicycle, and the phonograph for purposes of dictation, and he even played with something like an idea for motion pictures. Later in life, he was interested in

Fernsehen and the Teleharmonium, inventions that eventuated in the mixed blessings of television and continuously piped music. But he hardly mastered the typewriter or the bicycle, and he was even more inept in managing or financing inventions.

The great nightmare proved to be the Paige Typesetting Machine. As in other cases, Clemens was on the right track; his experience as a printer had taught him that a typesetter was the crying need of contemporary publishing. His reliance on "luck," however, blinded him to the visionary and impractical nature of Paige, and to the superiority of the rival Mergenthaler machine. As usually happened, his enthusiasm for the invention was boundless; in a letter to his brother he maintains:

> All the other wonderful inventions of the human brain sink pretty nearly into commonplace contrasted with this awful mechanical miracle. Telephones, telegraphs, locomotives, cotton gins, sewing machines, Babbage calculators, Jacquard looms, perfecting presses, Arkwright's frames—all mere toys, simplicities! The Paige Compositor marches alone and far in the lead of human inventions.[4]

Even after the invention had consumed $190,000, poured in at the rate of $3,000 a month, the perfectionist inventor still found new refinements to add. "Eventually—irony of fate—the Mergenthaler Company, so long scorned and derided, for twenty thousand dollars bought out the rights and assets and presented that marvelous work of genius, the mechanical wonder of the age, to the Sibley College of Engineering, where it is shown as the costliest piece of machinery, for its size, ever constructed." [5] Meanwhile, the Webster Company was deeper and deeper in debt because of the ruinous project to publish a *Library of American Literature*, and *A Connecticut Yankee in King Arthur's Court* (1889) and *The American Claimant* (1892) did little to recoup these losses. *Tom Sawyer Abroad* was the swan song of the Webster Company, which failed in the spring of 1894. From 1891 to 1895, the family lived in Europe, largely for economy, with Clemens scurrying back and forth across the ocean like a commuter. Clearly, all his frenzied travel did little to improve the situation until he met the Standard Oil executive, H. H. Rogers, long a Twain admirer, who kindly took Clemens' financial tangle into his capable hands. He saved the rights to the books, and helped map out a recovery program.

---

4 Paine, *Letters,* p. 508.
5 Albert Bigelow Paine, *Mark Twain, A Biography* (New York, Harper and Brothers, 1912), pp. 995–6.

Mrs. Clemens' own fortune was also involved, and she could not see financial failure as anything but moral disgrace; it was perhaps her influence that stimulated Clemens to such heroic efforts to repay his creditors in full. This he managed in four years, from the proceeds of a round-the-world lecture tour in 1895–96 and from its description in *Following the Equator* (1897). The lonely death of his beloved daughter Susy in 1896, while he and his wife and another daughter, Clara, were in Europe, plunged the family into protracted grief. They did not return to America until 1900, after an absence of nine years.

After the failure of the Webster Company, *Pudd'nhead Wilson* was published by the American Publishing Company in 1894, and *Joan of Arc* and *Tom Sawyer, Detective* in 1896 by Harpers, who obtained the rights for collected editions. Aside from his book on Christian Science, such shorter works as "The Man That Corrupted Hadleyburg," *What Is Man?* (printed privately in 1906), and various miscellaneous and reminiscent pieces, such as *The Mysterious Stranger,* there was little literary output in his later years. The death of Olivia in 1904 after a long illness and of his daughter Jean in 1909 simply confirmed the deepening pessimism that had marked his thought from much earlier. Temperamentally, though, he seemed to retain some spirit through the trip to England in 1907 to receive an honorary degree from Oxford, and various excursions to Bermuda. His last steady pleasure was interminable games of billiards with his biographer, Albert B. Paine. He died in 1910 of angina.

◈

This, then, is the general outline of Clemens' life. For a writer, however, we are also interested in a deeper dimension of experience, because we are better able to understand his creative achievement if we have a more detailed knowledge of his inner life. The kind of psychological adjustment he makes to this experience largely determines how the characters in his sketches and novels react to their experiences, and also how he represents reality even in his non-fiction. Consequently, a general view of the writer's personality and its expression in a metaphysic is inseparable from a more thorough consideration of his emotional and moral responses, both in his family and social relations, and also in his intellectual life.

Whatever the phrase "negative capability" may have meant to Keats, it certainly suggests to us now that one aspect of maturity is the power to live through one's ambivalent and contradictory drives. In this sense, Clemens attained an enviable kind of maturity, for despite the contradictions within his nature, and the anguish and despair that he occasionally vented, he remained a levelheaded and effective person as a husband, father, and public figure. He made good his financial failure without recourse to the bankruptcy laws; he stands as an abiding figure of irreverent and boyish fun who punctures false moral pretensions and monarchical sham; his *Huckleberry Finn* comes as close as any book to expressing the soul of our nation.

His brother, Orion, by contrast, was an unstable man who is said to have changed religion and political parties as much as three times in one day; given to sudden enthusiasms and short-lived but grandiose plans, he and his family were permanently dependent on Samuel's largess. Clemens caused those about him no such trouble, but there are countless indications that this emotional control was attained at a boyish level. If the laundering of his shirts did not please him, he would throw the offending garments, one after another, into a heap on the lawn under the bathroom window; he retained to the end a simple delight in gaudy costume and pageantry; he continually surrounded himself with young girls. In a sense like Lewis Carroll, he made a viable peace with his tensions that permitted him not only to live essentially as a child in a world of adults, but that encouraged creative exploitation of these very child-like impulses and reactions—even if the literary expression of these impulses was remarkably different in the two men.

The most sterling proof of his essential attitude is to be found in his works. The triumphs of boy-literature, *Huckleberry Finn* and *Tom Sawyer,* invariably inspire in readers countless vivid memories of their own childhood which they have forgotten or matured out of. *The Prince and the Pauper* and *Joan of Arc* are primarily successful as children's books. Clemens kept alive in his unconscious the whole climate of boyhood, intact and warm with life, and he transfers all its deepest rhythms and pulsations to the printed page. In revising *The Prince and the Pauper,* for example, Clemens not only sought mature literary judgments, but urged Howells and Edwin Pond Parker to read the manuscript to their children for their reactions.

Perhaps the deepest root of his later development is to be found in the Calvinism that Clemens imbibed in the Presbyterian Sunday School of Hannibal. He repeatedly fights grim battles, particularly in *The Mysterious Stranger*, with the character of a Providence who would arrange matters as badly as He obviously had. From a childhood attempt to pray for gingerbread all the way through to his fully developed philosophy in *What Is Man?* he was constantly rebelling against a view of the universe in which an arbitrary and capricious deity bungled unutterably. He always saw the "damned human race" as primary evidence of God's failure; he wrote to Howells, one of his dearest friends, "I suspect that to you there is still dignity in human life, & that Man is not a joke—a poor joke—the poorest that was ever contrived—an April-fool joke, played by a malicious Creator with nothing better to waste his time upon." [6] And his frequently expressed sympathy for the figure of Satan, which culminates in *The Mysterious Stranger,* reinforces this stand. His metaphysics, in one sense, is simply an extension of his humanitarian fulminations against secular injustices.

If he did not literally fear damnation, it was only because he could not accept conventional eschatology, as is demonstrated by *Extracts from Captain Stormfield's Visit to Heaven.* But this did not exonerate him from a sense of unworthiness which expressed itself in what we have already seen was a tender and easily aroused sense of guilt that took upon itself Herculean burdens of remorse. As a child, he saw all the town catastrophes as the elaborate means chosen by God to teach little Sam a sound moral lesson. On his wife's death, he excoriated his own religious skepticism because he thought it might have contributed to her heart condition. To an adult, the very next question would be guilt in the eyes of whom, or guilt in what kind of context of reward and punishment? But Clemens' professed theology, which we shall detail later, found no place for Biblical revelation or for standard anthropomorphic apologetics.

Driven, perhaps, by his sense of guilt Clemens took a deliberate pleasure in swearing, smoking, and generally misbehaving. The motive for his behavior is illustrated in an interchange with his wife who remarked " 'Youth dear, one does not act honorably for the sake of reward or even approbation.' " He answered " 'I do. I want payment in some coin for everything I do. If I can't get

---

[6] Henry Nash Smith and William M. Gibson, ed., *Mark Twain–Howells Letters* (Cambridge, Massachusetts, The Belknap Press of Harvard University Press, 1960), p. 689.

peace and joy in return for propping up my blatherskite of a crumbling soul, then—I'll let her rot and the quicker the better.' " [7]

This same reaction is exploited imaginatively in "The Facts Concerning a Recent Carnival of Crime in Connecticut," in which Mark Twain is confronted with a personification of his conscience as an ugly little dwarf covered with green mold. After an involved argument and comic chase, Twain strangles the impudent little monster, then gleefully launches on a two-week binge during which he burns a house that interrupts his view, takes a cow from a widow and some orphans, and murders thirty-eight persons in two weeks. Since his conscience had formerly tortured him on his treatment of tramps that came to the door, he closes thus:

> In conclusion I wish to state, by way of advertisement, that medical colleges desiring assorted tramps for scientific purposes, either by the gross, by cord measurement, or per ton, will do well to examine the lot in my cellar before purchasing elsewhere, as these were all selected and prepared by myself, and can be had at a low rate, because I wish to clear out my stock and get ready for the spring trade.

Clemens' rages were monumental; often they were exercised and sustained in excess of the objective provocation, whether it was an annoying noise or the piracy of his works or the colonial policy of King Leopold of Belgium. Sometimes the most gaudily pyrotechnic of the rages had no basis at all. After a three-week fury of preparing a vitriolic biography of editor Whitelaw Reid, because Clemens heard the *Tribune* had published regular attacks on him, he was prevailed upon to check the *Tribune*. He found the rumor groundless. His brilliant invective was also applied in the service of implacable grudges, such as this, revealed in one of his innumerable unmailed letters:

> Dear Sir: Oh—so you have arrived at last, but only by letter, I am sorry to say. I have long wanted to meet you, get acquainted with you and kill you. You wrote that thing about my lecture sixteen years ago, in the Jamestown, N.Y. Journal . . .[8]

---

[7] Clara Clemens, *My Father, Mark Twain* (New York, Harper and Brothers, 1931), p. 180.
[8] Clara Clemens, *My Father,* p. 69.

The obverse of excessive rage is excessive sentimentality, where sweetness replaces violence. As an example, throughout his mature life we find him indulging in an adulation for pure young women, adequately reflected in his reverent and pious feeling for Joan of Arc. In 1875 he organized in Hartford a Saturday Morning Club for girls from sixteen to twenty who heard a variety of speakers on cultural and intellectual subjects. This was followed by the Juggernaut, an international correspondence club for young ladies of which he is the only male member, and in a later club of "Angel Fish," founded during one of his sojourns in Bermuda, for which he selected the candidates. These clubs were accompanied by the elaborate imaginative clap-trap which children usually contrive.

This sentimentality parallels his fussy moral responses, particularly in the area of sexual behavior. In public moral questions, he was always punctilious, notably in his taking firm stands against the alleged adultery of Henry Ward Beecher and the actual adultery of Gogol. There is a well-known absence of any hint of sexuality in his writing, aside from the miscegenation theme in *Pudd'nhead Wilson.* Even the relatively innocent aspect of adolescent curiosity in Tom Sawyer's surprising Becky as she peruses a naked human figure in an anatomy book was censored before it reached print. It is the more curious in a writer who is so often thought of as a figure of the wide-open frontier that a taboo on sexual reference should operate so thoroughly. It is not a lack of knowledge or interest or a perversion of any kind that stands at the bottom of this. Walter Blair sees this trait as a simple moral assumption of contemporary society. In *1601,* the ribald transcription of a conversation that could never have occurred at the court of Elizabeth I, we have simply the equivalent of looking at dirty pictures behind the barn, made all the more piquant because it delighted Rev. Joseph H. Twichell, Clemens' long-time friend in Hartford. And it is something like a small boy's idea of Paris that would lead him to address the Stomach Club of that city on onanism. In private conversation with a sensational lady novelist of his day, he apparently expressed advanced notions of sexual morality, but sternly forbade her to make any of his remarks public, just as he never made public his approval of Grover Cleveland's having had a mistress.

In relation to his family, he never outgrew the simplicity of response that a child makes to praise or honors at school. To his mother, to his friend Mrs. Fairbanks, and to his wife, he proudly relayed all the flattering remarks or praise he received; his only regret about the Oxford degree was that Livy was not alive to appreciate the honor.

Van Wyck Brooks has pointed out the mother role of Olivia in their married relation, and there are countless anecdotes about how she and her daughters "dusted off" papa after he had committed this or that social blunder. Eventually the family developed a code of signals to warn him that he should talk more or less, should pay more attention to the lady on his right, and the like. It is said that if Olivia failed to notice infractions, his young daughters, hiding behind a screen, prompted her to prompt him. And his response to surveillance was that of a boy: swearing in the bathroom where he thinks he cannot be heard, but almost unconsciously willing to be overheard, for the delicious sense of disapproval and final reconciliation with Olivia.

From this situation, it is hardly a step over to the habit of submitting the day's manuscript to Olivia and the girls for their approval. Whether he or Olivia read aloud, or whether she edited silently with her pencil, nearly everything he wrote after his marriage (and *The Innocents Abroad* during his courtship) passed for her approval. The fact that he did not confide in her before he delivered the Whittier birthday speech only confirmed her authority in his eyes. In later years, he even purposefully planted passages that he knew Livy would disapprove of solely for the pleasure of being reproved and then arguing over the issue with the unwitting support of his daughters. He took inordinate pleasure in carrying his point, and then secretly rubbing out the offending passage anyway. During periods when her eyes were weak, Olivia insisted that William Dean Howells peruse manuscripts before publication in order to excise any indelicacies.

Few people would any longer accept the thesis that Olivia and Howells emasculated Sam's virile prose or strapped him into a straight-jacket of puritan propriety. It is clear that he wanted her approval, if only because we find him on the *Quaker City* cruise submitting his manuscript to "Mother" Fairbanks, the wife of a part owner of the Cleveland *Herald*. Thus even before he had seen the miniature of Olivia, he sought out matronly sanction, and the testimony of other passengers is that Mrs. Fairbanks found a fair amount unacceptable. Whole sheaves of manuscript were torn up and thrown into the water. He ends several early letters to Mrs. Fairbanks with the mock-serious plea "Give me another sermon!"

Clemens was distinguished by a notorious eccentricity of dress, running from the seedily unkempt miner's outfit that he wore into the *Enterprise* office to the scarlet Oxford robes he wore for his daughter Clara's wedding. At various times he sported string ties that distressed his wife, lavender gloves, pink and green socks, and in later years he dressed entirely in white. He horrified Charles Langdon by his sloppiness when he arrived as a house guest in Elmira, and Mrs. Thomas Bailey Aldrich pointedly refused to announce dinner while he was in the house because she assumed, from his normal dress and manner, that he was drunk. The family servant, Katy Leary, testifies that Clemens delighted in wearing night shirts which she decorated in pink and red and blue.

❧ ☙

Clemens began his serious reading as a pilot, with sporadic attempts to learn French. Just before this, in Cincinnati, he had been fired with intellectual excitement by a chance meeting at his boarding house with a Scotsman named McFarlane, whose ideas on evolution, so Clemens says, inspirited him with the germ of the deterministic pessimism to which he held more and more staunchly as he aged. McFarlane said the whole glorious process of evolution eventuated in man, a mean and dirty creature whose reason only enabled him to be more base than the subsidiary creatures who preceded him.

Clemens read year after year the same favorites: *The Mutineers of the Bounty,* Pepys' *Diary, Two Years Before the Mast,* a book on the Andes, Dumas, Lecky's *History of European Morals,* and Andrew D. White's *A History of the Warfare of Science with Theology.* His most enduring loves were St. Simon's *Memoirs* (which he is said to have read twenty times), Suetonius' *Lives of the Caesars,* Malory's *Morte d'Arthur,* and Carlyle on the French Revolution. For the rest, the list consists of a varied and undistinguished lot, chosen for personal interest or because he knew the authors. He professed to hate the work of Jane Austen heartily, and preferred *A Tale of Two Cities* of all Dickens' works; he reserved particular spite for Scott, Eliot, James, and Meredith. Olivia was once thoroughly embarrassed by having to reply to an inquirer that her husband had no opinion on "Balzac, Thackeray, and the rest" because he had never read them. This general distaste for novels—except those of William Dean Howells, whose work he praised extravagantly—led him to prefer books of fact, biography, history, and memoirs. In poetry, his taste ran to Browning, Kipling, and Omar Khayyám. He also felt great sympathy with eighteenth-century writers such as Paine, Voltaire, and Goldsmith, whom he read in his early piloting days. It is almost certain that their deism shaped his early thinking.

Although he took strong political stands from time to time, as in his Mugwump enthusiasm of 1884, politics did not interest him very continuously, partially because of his extended visits abroad. He was violently antimonarchical (except when royalty paid personal court to him), and his aim as a writer is always insistently democratic:

> Indeed I have been misjudged, from the very first. I have never tried in even one single instance, to help cultivate the cultivated classes. I was not equipped for it, either by native gifts or training. And I never had any ambition in that direction, but always hunted for bigger game—the masses. I have seldom deliberately tried to instruct them, but have done my best to entertain them. To simply amuse them would have satisfied my dearest ambition at any time; for they could get instruction elsewhere, and I had two chances to help to the teacher's one: for amusement is a good preparation for study and a good healer of fatigue after it. My audience is dumb, it has no voice in print, and so I cannot know whether I have won its approbation or only got its censure.[9]

He appears to have been fairly well informed on world affairs, although his sense of public propriety sometimes prevented his saying what he thought, or even prompted him to say the opposite. This was particularly true in regard to England's role in the Boer War. While he deplored her actions in this particular crisis, he felt England had to be supported as the last bastion of civilization and personal liberty in Europe.

He had a youthful weakness for fads and cure-alls, which goes along with the more harmless delight in parades and pageants that he retained even in old age. Immediately following the collapse of the Webster Company and the Paige interests, he became enthusiastic about a carpet-pattern weaver; Plasmon, a skim milk product; osteopathy; a patented cash register; and a patented spiral hatpin. His spirited defense of a Professor Loisette's killingly intricate system for improving the memory anticipated his later interest in the use of shorthand for alphabet reform. When he approached literature, it was always with the wildly partisan heat of his attack on Cooper or his defense of Harriet Shelley, or

---

[9] Paine, *Letters,* pp. 527–8.

the intellectually disgraceful insistence that Bacon wrote Shakespeare's plays.

Samuel Clemens' religious beliefs can be briefly summarized in his own words, in excerpts from a notebook entry made in the early eighties which his biographer assures us remained essentially his creed:

> I believe in God the Almighty.
>
> I do not believe He has ever sent a message to man by anybody, or delivered one to him by word of mouth, or made Himself visible to mortal eyes at any time in any place.
>
> I believe that the Old and New Testaments were imagined and written by man, and that no line in them was authorized by God, much less inspired by Him. . . .
>
> I do not believe in special providences. I believe that the universe is governed by strict and immutable laws. If one man's family is swept away by a pestilence and another man's is spared it is only the law working: God is not interfering in that small matter, either against the one man or in favor of the other. . . .
>
> I believe that the world's moral laws are the outcome of the world's experience. It needed no God to come down out of heaven to tell men that murder and theft and the other immoralities were bad, both for the individual who commits them and for society which suffers from them.
>
> If I break all these moral laws I cannot see how I injure God by it, for He is beyond the reach of injury by me—I could as easily injure a planet by throwing mud at it. . . .[10]

Along with these ideas, he expresses perplexity about a state of being after death, although he refuses to think that if there be such a state it has anything to do with reward and punishment. In summary, the credo seems to be a compound of eighteenth-century deism and Higher Criticism. The rationalism was undoubtedly supported by Clemens' informal but absorbed interest in astronomy and geology, studies he pursued throughout his life. This rationalism is balanced, however, by an equally strong interest in the milder fringes of psychic phenomena and mental telepathy. The only religious observances in his life, aside from the Sunday School of his youth, were the family prayers and Bible readings instituted by Olivia on their marriage, which he soon refused to carry on. Although the Clemenses rented a pew at Rev. Joseph H. Twichell's Hartford Church, they never became members.

[10] Paine, *Biography*, p. 1583.

There remain his famous determinism and pessimism which have come to be as integrally associated with him in the public mind as his Missouri boyhood. Clemens felt, in adapting McFarlane's pre-Darwinian evolutionary theory, that the tiniest of seemingly inconsequential occurrences was determined by an inescapable chain of causes leading back to the first energies of the primal atom. He felt this deeply and he illuminated his conviction by vivid description and elaboration. He was equally firm in his defense of a crude kind of psychological determinism based on the assumption that no one has ever held any original idea that did not come to him from some environmental source. Later he read Darwin (perhaps after hearing that Darwin read Twain!) and this undoubtedly confirmed many of these beliefs. The determinism is maintained with the kind of tenacity and profundity that may indicate that the belief is a psychic necessity. There is little doubt that his highly sensitive conscience demanded this release from responsibility, and his renunciation of an eschatology of reward-and-punishment would conveniently lead to a renunciation of personal accountability. Of course in the moments of grief, when he heaped recriminatory coals on his own head for the death of Henry or Langdon, he did not invoke this determinism.

Perhaps the bridge between the guilt and the determinism is, mentally, simply a matter of imagery. Clemens delighted in Swift's habit of magnifying the tiny, or shrinking the immense—this was one of the distinct pleasures he drew from astronomy. He repeatedly sees our world or mankind as microbes in the body of a huge deity. One of the most extravagant of his unfinished fantasies is an elaboration of this idea called "3000 Years Among the Microbes." When he saw himself as guilty of enormous crimes, he was magnifying his importance in the scheme of things. And when he minimized human scale, he found the solace of not counting, of being an infinitesimal blob in a huge liquid process that went immutably on despite whatever he thought or did.

The pessimism, then, is an easy derivative from this position, although it apparently co-existed in his temperament from an early date. If life is as totally meaningless as this vision suggests, then the bitter aphorisms we shall find in *Pudd'nhead Wilson* are totally justified, and death is the inestimable boon that he calls it.

We see Clemens, then, as an effectively matured person in terms of his society, one who got along in the business of living as well as the next one, carried along on a tide of social conviviality. But this maturity is at a youthful level in which the temper tantrums, the tenaciously held ideas, and the constant surveillance and correction of refined females take their places in the pattern.

In summary, his career is perfectly representative of a young and developing culture which, if it were to be "made" at all, had to be self-made, a culture which was as crude as the terrain and the conditions imposed on it, a culture which was as money-conscious as its own developing wealth inevitably made it, a culture which needed to be informal because it was still seeking its forms. Indeed, countless Europeans, and many Americans as well, still see the American male as most adequately symbolized in Hemingway's Francis Macomber or in Fitzgerald's Jay Gatsby—the "great American boy-men" full of vitality and irrepressible dreams, measuring themselves against a narrow but refining matriarchy concentrated in Eastern seaboard culture.

While we have only spoken of Clemens' dour philosophy as a result of psychological factors, it may be far more valuable as a cultural storm signal than most critics have realized. If the intellectual assertion of determinism and pessimism has some relation to the inherent weaknesses and delusions of the "boy-men," then Clemens has unconsciously performed a major service of cultural evaluation which needs to be taken to heart.

To have bridged these cultures, to have lived with these tensions, and at the same time to have delighted the countless multitudes of readers throughout the world as he did with his attempts to articulate these tensions, is a distinct achievement, and a completely American one.

2

THE WRITER

THE PERVASIVE role of tradition, within which any writer of artistic significance must work out his destiny, is emphasized in T. S. Eliot's "Tradition and the Individual Talent." It is the tradition that provides him with the conventions of style and structure and content which make up his fundamental working material. The great writer, nevertheless, transcends that very tradition by using it for more profound, more subtle, or more all-encompassing purposes than did his literary forebears. Samuel Clemens is just such a genius. As Kenneth S. Lynn proves convincingly in *Mark Twain and Southwestern Humor,* Clemens inherited a long tradition dating back ultimately to pre-Revolutionary days. It is a tradition of political conservatism and gentlemanly style, heavily indebted to the example of Joseph Addison, in which humor is employed to support the values of the Whig party in its revulsion at the leveling tendencies of Jacksonian Democrats. In the series of crises in Southern life that led to the Civil War, the gentlemanly Southwestern humorists (of what we could today call the South-Central area) began by satirizing the vulgarity, ignorance, and barbarism of the Jacksonian element. These character sketches surveyed this horror with gentlemanly calm and style from the safe distance of a "frame" narration. But as the Whig values were lost in the frenzy of secession, the vernacular style, that had heretofore been used only sparingly, became the idiom for the now demoralized gentleman. By a curious transference, he capitulated to the style of his unscrupulous enemy, whom he now saw overrunning society. This tradition works itself out in William T. Porter's *Spirit of the Times,* a sporting journal that printed many of these pieces, and in the individual volumes of Augustus Baldwin Longstreet, Johnson J. Hooper, Thomas Bangs Thorpe, Joseph G. Baldwin, Richard Malcolm Johnston, and George Washington Harris. Clemens came to adulthood, both as a person and as a writer, at the time these traditions reached a shattering crisis in the Civil War. During his apprenticeship as a printer and later as a newspaper man in Nevada, Sam Clemens tried his hand at most of the stylistic, structural, and topical effects of this school of writers; he mastered these effects, and he transcended them by using them in what must be seen as a literary and a spiritual triumph. Above all, by projecting these now subtilized techniques into *Huckleberry Finn,* he enriched the form of the novel.

It is no reflection on this triumph that the novel, as a tradition, was a dead issue for Clemens. He claimed to detest this form of writing, and did not read widely in the field himself. In 1885 he told Howells that he "nearly died from the overwork" of trying to read George Eliot's *Middlemarch.* He got through three chapters of *Daniel Deronda,* "losing flesh all the time." He continues:

> I can't stand George Eliot and Hawthorne and those people; I see what they are at a hundred years before they get to it and they just tire me to death. And as for 'The Bostonians,' I would rather be damned to John Bunyan's heaven than read that.[1]

For Clemens is, fundamentally, a humorist. This explains his enormous success as a lecturer and after-dinner speaker, and the endearing qualities that made him so lovable as a father, friend, and commentator on current affairs. He is the apotheosis of a kind of urbanely folksy wisdom whose subtlety, complexity, and moral purpose could only find expression in humor.

◈ ◈

To be sure, Clemens himself occasionally denied his calling. During his courtship he wrote to "Mother" Fairbanks, asking her to help convince Olivia of his true nature: "—poor girl, anybody who could convince her that I was not a humorist would secure her eternal gratitude! She thinks a humorist is something perfectly

---

[1] Albert Bigelow Paine, ed., *Mark Twain's Letters* (New York, Harper and Brothers, 1911), pp. 454–5.

awful." [2] The reason that a large number of people thought this in Clemens' day is easily supplied by Howells:

> Except the political humorists, like Mr. Lowell—if there are any like him—the American humorists formerly chose the wrong in public matters; they were on the side of slavery, of drunkenness, and of irreligion; the friends of civilization were their prey; their spirit was thoroughly vulgar and base. Before 'John Phoenix,' there was scarcely any American humorist—not of the distinctly literary sort—with whom one could smile and keep one's self respect. [3]

But as Kenneth S. Lynn points out, both Howells and Olivia were ironically in error here; this tradition began with the most elegant of gentlemanly aims, and was very strongly committed to temperance. It was in the holocaust of the Civil War that these values were lost, and it was the writings of Mark Twain that proved to be the apotheosis of the tradition, holding in suspension a complex mixture of the traits of Southwestern Humor.

What Clemens shared with the earlier funnymen was a method, and although more hardy minds than ours have balked at defining this method, we can at least distinguish its major outlines. Gertrude Stein hit on the essence of the matter when she remarked "How can anything be different from what it is. I do not know any such a thing. Very many are knowing this. I am not knowing this." Miss Stein is obviously very seriously perplexed by the contrast between what is actually true and what most people assume to be true. She is perplexed by the difference between appearance and reality, or, more acutely, the difference between the delusions we usually accept unthinkingly, and the real basis of those delusions.

Now a humorist simply exaggerates or heightens the contrast between illusion and reality to a point where the contrast becomes so ludicrously extreme as to be laughable. As an example, take Clemens' definition of Thanksgiving:

> . . . a function which originated in New England two or three centuries ago when those people recognized that they really had something to be thankful for—annually, not oftener—if they had succeeded in exterminating their neighbors, the Indians, during the previous twelve months instead of getting exterminated by their neighbors, the Indians. Thanksgiving Day became a habit, for the reason that in the course of time, the exterminating had ceased to

[2] Dixon Wecter, ed., *Mark Twain to Mrs. Fairbanks* (San Marino, California, Huntington Library, 1949), p. 63.
[3] William Dean Howells, *My Mark Twain* (New York, Harper and Brothers, 1910), p. 138.

be mutual and was all on the white man's side, consequently on the Lord's side. . . .[4]

The mechanism by which the discrepancy is presented is, of course, irony. The speaker says something different from what he actually means—either by understatement, by overstatement, or by any other conceivable degree of indirection. Obviously Clemens is saying that Thanksgiving, in Gertrude Stein's phrase, is different from what it is—it is assumed to be a pious and righteous holiday; in his exasperation at the delusion involved in this view, Clemens goes over to the opposite extreme of saying it represents gratitude that we murdered more of them than they did of us.

The deliciousness of the effect is the audience's discovery of the degree of difference between what was actually said and what was meant. To this irony of statement may be added irony of manner. Characteristically, Clemens presents his amusement with a poker face, so that the reader's discovery of the discrepancy is accompanied by the explosion of laughter, since the reader realizes all at once both the discrepancy itself and the added discrepancy of Clemens' mock-serious presentation. As he says, ". . . the humorous writer pretends to absolute seriousness (when he knows his trade). . . ." This manner is deeply imbedded in his experience, since he tells us that in childhood he learned such tricks of delivery from his mother, a master at this device.

As Clemens encountered this irony in Southwestern humor, it took two major forms, profanity and the tall tale, both forms of exaggeration. In swearing, one invokes the concern of the Deity in a petty matter which could hardly interest Him (overstatement); or else, in allied forms of strong language, one exaggerates without invoking the Deity, as when Clemens stormed at an officious proofreader: ". . . he couldn't puke his ignorant impudence over *my* punctuation, I wouldn't allow it for a moment." The tall tale, too, derives its effect from the discrepancy between the literal truth and the ironic extension of that truth in an effort to accommodate it to the intense feelings of the speaker. For one thing, frontiersmen joked about the rigor, danger, loneliness, and crudity of their way of life as a means of whistling in the dark, of laughing away terror and depression. By exaggerating the conditions of life, reality did not seem so overwhelming. Secondly, as Lynn demonstrates, they were also showing off for the mannered European and Eastern

4 *Mark Twain's Autobiography,* Stormfield Edition (New York, Harper and Brothers, 1929), Vol. i, pp. 291–2.

tourists who expected to find brutality and vulgarity, so the frontiersmen gave them a bit more than they bargained for.

The most obvious immediate deduction to be drawn from this definition is that although it involves laughter, humor need not necessarily be regarded as frivolous or vulgar—as apparently Olivia regarded it during the courtship. The Thanksgiving definition shows that humor is capable of treating serious and practical subjects in a serious and practical way. In Clemens' statement, quoted in chapter one, about his aiming to entertain, not to instruct, the masses, he presents one point of view. In the following statement, he presents its opposite:

> There are those who say a novel should be a work of art solely, and you must not preach in it, you must not teach in it. That may be true as regards novels but it is not true as regards humor. Humor must not professedly teach, and it must not professedly preach, but it must do both if it would live forever. By forever, I mean thirty years. . . .
>
> I have always preached. That is the reason that I have lasted thirty years. If the humor came of its own accord and uninvited, I have allowed it a place in my sermon, but I was not writing the sermon for the sake of the humor. I should have written the sermon just the same, whether any humor applied for admission or not.[5]

(Clemens' early training in humorous newspaper squibs, letters, and editorials had long-term consequences in his continuing inability to organize plots, chains of thought, or any kind of ordered rational sequence, except in novels where humor is absent or subsidiary. The joke basis does not permit very great length. In the standard form, the springing of the discrepancy is reserved for the punch line, in order to preserve suspense. In other forms, where suspense is not the primary objective, the discrepancy may be announced earlier and then elaborated upon. The joke may be very brief, as when Clemens says of a club that "it always had more clergymen in it than good people." Joke may burgeon into anecdote, and anecdote into episode, but there it reaches its own natural limitations. For a work of greater length, all one can do is string separate jokes together. Howells sees this clearly:

> I, for instance, in putting this paper together, am anxious to observe some sort of logical order, to discipline such impressions and notions as I have of the subject into a coherent body which shall

5 Bernard DeVoto, ed., *Mark Twain in Eruption* (New York, Harper and Brothers, 1940), pp. 202–3.

march columnwise to a conclusion obvious if not inevitable from the start. But Mr. Clemens, if he were writing it, would not be anxious to do any such thing. He would take whatever offered itself to his hand out of that mystical chaos, that divine ragbag, which we call the mind, and leave the reader to look after relevancies and sequences for himself. These there might be, but not of that hard-and-fast sort which I am eager to lay hold of, and the result would at least be satisfactory to the author, who would have shifted the whole responsibility to the reader, with whom it belongs, at least as much as with the author.[6]

This shifting of responsibility to the reader is why it is criminal to explain a joke: the pleasure involved is the reader's creative discovery for himself that there are multiple discrepancies built into the statement.

Now if humor itself is to be his metier, the next most important step for Clemens was the projection of certain personal traits into the artificial—but intensely real—nature of Mark Twain.

In traditional Southwestern humor, the Whig gentleman spoke in his own person in the frame narration; he projected the traits of the Jacksonian rabble into Ransy Sniffle, Flan Sucker, Sammy Stonestreet, Simon Suggs, and similar brutal, unprincipled yokels. With the appearance of George Washington Harris's Sut Lovingood, however, the transfer is all but complete, and the vernacular style and point of view of the triumphant Democratic rabble have become those of the author in a pseudonymous projection. This tradition continued through the era of the professional funnyman, often a lecturer, in the figures of Artemus Ward, Petroleum V. Nasby, John Phoenix, Dan de Quille, and many others. These pseudonymous projections became symbolic vehicles or comic masks that presented the author's personality in an exaggerated or intensified form, an ironic pose.

The need for such a projection stands in direct relation to the aspirations of the writer for *artistic* success. Aristotle has clearly shown that history deals in facts, but that art deals in probabilities. If these humorists transcribed their experiences literally, they would be presenting something close to history. They knew intuitively, however, that their province was art, and that the ends of art are best realized by an impersonality, a freedom from the shackles of fact, which takes them invariably into a realm of probability. To put it another way (again, as Aristotle says), fact is tied down to one time and one place, whereas probability is

[6] *My Mark Twain,* p. 167.

universal—and immortal art always possesses at least this quality of universality, or applicability to many persons' experience. In short, if the humorist, for purposes of irony, is to tell preposterous tales, then they are more "probable" if they come from the mouth of a preposterous person.

Clemens sought this pseudonymous objectivity in his development, probably completely unconscious of all the implications we find in the process. His early efforts in newspapers were signed with such pseudonyms as "W. Epaminodas Adrastus Blab," "Grumbler," "Rambler," "Peter Pencilcase's Son, John Snooks," "Josh," "Thomas Jefferson Snodgrass," and "Quintus Curtius Snodgrass." The characters behind these fictitious names are usually the standard ones of the crude and vulgar yokel in his first clashes with civilization, or of the supercilious and bumptious editor.

The pseudonym of Mark Twain was first used in his reports for the *Virginia City Territorial Enterprise* concerning sittings of the Nevada Legislature. Even after this, however, we find the convention of the pseudonymous companion—"Unreliable," Mr. Larryndor Kidd, John William Skae, and the irrepressible Mr. Brown of the Hawaiian and European travel correspondence. In part, these characters are foils, to make Twain's sophistication and worldliness show to greater advantage. They are often vestigial frontiersmen, scapegoats for all the concern with vomiting, stinks, overeating, vulgar dress and manners and poor taste that Clemens wants to treat, but without involving the figure of Twain himself. In later works, we find Clemens treating actual friends under thinly veiled pseudonyms and giving them, too, slightly exaggerated qualities that make them figures of art rather than of reality.

But more importantly, they are a kind of branching out of the writer's personality into an *alter ego*. This habit runs through his work like the rich leads of ore that he describes in the Nevada mountains; it blossoms into the Jekyll and Hyde short story "Edward Mills and George Benton," into something approaching identical twins in *The Prince and the Pauper,* into the Siamese variety in "Those Extraordinary Twins," and into that ultimate Quixote-Panza dichotomy in Huck and Tom.

The Mark Twain characteristics, however, settle into a blend of those personal traits of Clemens (now including, with some judicious expurgations, even the nastier tastes of Mr. Brown) which are consonant with the public figure he wants to present.

The Mark Twain figure is by-and-large a naive, incompetent,

lazy shirker, the one who rides in the wagon when the others walk, or who steers the boat instead of rowing it. When he does exercise a skill, such as in his piloting days, it is one dependent on keenness and sensitivity of observation and memory. It is also, incidentally, a position of glory that feeds his large vanity. His great projects of claiming timber land on Lake Tahoe or mining silver or tracking the mysterious Mr. Whiteman to his fabulously rich "cement mine" always end up in a loafing and fishing expedition. In his lack of practical skills, such as tying up a pack horse, he is always the drone and the parasite of the group. But he loves to talk and to listen (and, with somewhat reduced enthusiasm, to write). When he accidentally starts a ruinous forest fire, he calmly uses it for several paragraphs of purple prose.

As Clemens himself ages, the figure of Mark Twain changes little. During his travels in Germany, Switzerland, Australia, and India there is a dulling of the sense of pristine adventure; in its place, one more often finds the *longueurs* of the raconteur.

He is a keen observer who exercises a tender sense of justice on the phenomena he sees. He is, heart and soul, a prevaricator who plays with reality as does a child with a hunk of clay—flattening, lumping, stretching, and tearing it at will until it assumes an outrageous shape. The sum of these characteristics is an organically whole personality, in which the vanity does not prevent his admitting to substantial weaknesses, or in which the weaknesses do not cripple his sense of his own worth. The prevarication, however, is the nucleus of the whole organism; it is the looseness of his sense of accuracy which permits Clemens to project this lovable and genial personality of Mark Twain into the books. It is no accident, of course, that the laziness, impracticality, cowardice, and other such weaknesses are characteristic of most humorists' pseudonymous or artistically projected personalities—for instance Robert Benchley or James Thurber in our own day. The humorist in this sense continues the role of the medieval jester, a person whose life work is to profess human weakness, but, by warming it in his heart, to make of it a human triumph.

The most salutary result of glancing at very early writings is to see how far Clemens advanced as he matured. In gross terms, he began—like his early pseudonymous masks—as a gauche, fairly vulgar provincial, and each new set of letters reveals a breadth of experience and reference which frees him from certain crudities by almost mathematical increments. At each step of the progression, however, either through a happy accident of fate or else by the natural course of development, he is provincial within larger and larger contexts—from Keokuk, Iowa, to St. Louis and Cincinnati, to New Orleans, to Nevada, to San Francisco and the whole Pacific coast.

As a typesetter on Orion's Hannibal *Journal,* he provided miscellaneous material. When he began his ambitious trip to the sources of the Amazon, he contracted with the Keokuk *Daily Post* to provide travel letters at $5.00 each, which he meant ultimately to collect as a book to be called "Snodgrass Dierrea." As far as we know, this agreement resulted in the three "Thomas Jefferson Snodgrass" letters of October, 1856, from St. Louis, and of November, 1856, and April, 1857, from Cincinnati.[7] They record the experiences of the yokel at a performance of Shakespeare's *Julius Caesar,* which begin with his rendition of "Auld Lang Syne" on a comb, and end in his being ejected from the theater for making a disturbance. The incidents are related in the dialect that so delighted contemporary humorists. The second letter, about a train ride from Keokuk to Cincinnati, and the third, in which Snodgrass is left with a bawling abandoned infant, are in the same style, whose distinguishing mark is the use of country metaphors.

This approach had to be modified sooner or later because the extreme provinciality of the narrator forces Clemens to make these pieces into character sketches to the exclusion of objective reporting. The effort of describing a train as it appears for the first time to an untutored bumpkin, leaves little space to say much of any inherent interest about trains or travel. Probably Mr. Brown was eventually abandoned for the same reason. Certainly, as Clemens' horizons expanded, the very effort of filtering complex reality through the barrier of a chuckleheaded narrator must have proved onerous.

The ten letters of Quintus Curtius Snodgrass that appeared in the New Orleans *Daily Crescent* from January through March of 1861 are attributed to Clemens on strong internal evidence, although they seem to indicate that the writer saw some military service in Louisiana, which Clemens himself never mentioned.[8] A military expedition to Baton Rouge, an imaginary dinner with

[7] Charles Honce, ed., *The Adventures of Thomas Jefferson Snodgrass* (Chicago, Pascal Covici, 1928).

[8] Ernest E. Leisy, ed., *The Letters of Quintus Curtius Snodgrass* (Dallas, Southern Methodist University Press, 1946).

Olivia Clemens

President Lincoln, a military ball, and a gastronomical spree in New Orleans are combined with a mock manual of advice to green soldiers. The dialect has given way to Dickensian and classical allusions and the French and Latin phrases stick out like sore thumbs.[9] He has made an immense stride forward in the technique of humor, since he is obviously trying his wings in the devices of understatement. The touch is rude, particularly at the punch line, where the reader feels he is being prodded so he won't miss the point, and the obsessive use of understatement becomes monotonous.

These letters are addressed to Mr. Brown, who will himself show up in later travel correspondence; at the moment, the narrator's companion is Mr. Larryndor Kidd, a vulgar and uncouth person who wolfs down tons of food at a sitting.

Between these letters and the Sandwich Islands excursion lay perhaps the greatest literary watershed of his career. The reporting and letters to the *Territorial Enterprise* of Virginia City from 1862 to 1864 represent a crucial state in his evolution.[10] It was at this point that he strongly modified the "character sketch" approach, and consequently gained in objectivity. This newspaper service also closed the final door against crude dialect. Since reporting facts gave little leeway for artistic elaboration, this period of his life might pass, in part, as a disciplinary trial by fire. But one glance at what he wrote as a reporter shows that the unbuttoned, wide-open atmosphere of Nevada journalism permitted him plenty of room to stretch his arms, scratch himself, belch, and generally relax his way through reporting. The conventions of tall talk, of journalistic hoaxes (such as the petrified man and the bloody massacre that Clemens invented to fill a dearth in news), and of inter-paper rivalries, exercised his imagination thoroughly. Nevertheless, as a parliamentary reporter for the sittings of the Territorial Legislature and Constitutional Convention, his newspaper kept after him to supply facts, such as a record of who voted for and against various proposals, which he found more than a little annoying.

---

9 Clemens nowhere else shows these stylistic traits (except of Harris's report of a journey early in Volume 2 of *Roughing It,* which is sprinkled with foreign phrases for comic purposes). Certainly never again does he show such a knowledge of Dickens. This, to my mind, is the puzzling element in the attribution, although other traits of Clemens come through clearly enough.

10 Henry Nash Smith and Frederick Anderson, eds., *Mark Twain of the Enterprise* (Berkeley and Los Angeles, University of California Press, 1957); and the same editors' *Mark Twain: San Francisco Virginia City Territorial Enterprise Correspondent* (San Francisco, The Book Club of California, 1957).

He continues his vulgar *alter ego* in the person of "Unreliable," a nickname for Clement T. Rice, reporter for the Virginia City *Daily Union,* a good friend who was extremely reliable in reporting facts. "Unreliable" crashes parties, sometimes in outrageously ill-fitting borrowed or stolen clothes, and eats and drinks his way through enough provisions to supply an army.

⌊There are other standard comic devices which Clemens initiates in these days. A favorite stylistic device is to describe one phenomenon in a vocabulary taken from another context, as when he treats a Virginia reel in military terminology, or a wedding in the language of articles of incorporation for mines.⌉Repetition for irritatingly "shaggy dog" purposes, a device he uses in later books, appears here in William Stewart's speeches on the criminality of taxing mines, which recur with maddening frequency in the proceedings of the mock "Third House" of the Legislature. His current indulgence in the reforming diatribe is directed at a Carson City undertaker who charges high prices.

During his days in California, Clemens was both more and less free than in Nevada. The *Morning Call* required a severer discipline of punctuality, steadiness, and sobriety of material, but at the same time, he contributed literary pieces first to the *Golden Era* and later to the *Californian* (edited by Bret Harte and Charles Henry Webb). In his pieces for the *Era* (which appeared even before he left Nevada) we find him indulging, among other things, in his bloody-minded delight in violence. A kind of masochistic interest in anatomical and physiological scatology, in corpses and putrefaction, seems to be standard equipment for many humorists —from Aristophanes and Petronius down through Swift and Sterne to Aldous Huxley and Evelyn Waugh. Such material was also, of course, a staple of the Southwestern tradition. In terms of our theory of discrepancies, we can see that these gruesome details serve as counter-allegations against any assumption that life is pretty, calm, or sweet; such was the purpose of the early Whig gentleman who felt, nevertheless, that some of the amenities could be salvaged.

Mark Twain, at this point in his life, was learning to handle this material technically, although his aims appear to have been mixed. In "Those Blasted Children," he simply gives vent to personal exasperation at the brats who play in his hallway by suggesting "cures" for them that outdistance anything mentioned in "A Modest Proposal." He ends with prescriptions for various methods of cooking them, or sawing off the lower jaw to prevent stuttering. The climax of this violent kind of horror is "The Great Prize Fight," in which two California gubernatorial candidates literally tear each other to shreds. At one of the minor climaxes of the battle, Governor Low "sent one of his ponderous fists crashing through his opponent's ribs and in among his vitals, and instantly afterward he hauled out poor Stanford's left lung and smacked him in the face with it." Stanford, in reply, "jumped at his old speciality, Gov. Low's head [which he had already rendered nearly unrecognizable]; he tore it loose from his body and knocked him down with it." [11] The fight goes on from there.

Even in ladies' fashions, on which there are a number of satirical pieces, the same spirit prevails:

> Miss R. P., with that repugnance to ostentation in dress which is so peculiar to her, was attired in a simple white lace collar, fastened with a neat pearl-button solitaire. The fine contrast between the sparkling vivacity of her natural optic and the steadfast attentiveness of her placid glass eye was the subject of general and enthusiastic remark. . . .
>
> Miss C. L. B. had her fine nose elegantly enameled, and the easy grace with which she blew it from time to time, marked her as a cultivated and accomplished woman of the world; its exquisitely modulated tone excited the admiration of all who had the happiness to hear it.[12]

The intricate and labyrinthine nonsense of his diction in describing fabrics and stitching warms the hearts of any men who have ever wandered by mistake into the women's page of yesterday's newspaper.

The great triumph of this period is the "Celebrated Jumping Frog" yarn, the piece that first brought him national fame. It incorporates all the best in Clemens' colloquial style, in his gentle wisdom of human nature, and in the elaborate complexity of his sure and fine comic effects. In addition, it is, in its limited scope, the culminating jewel in the tradition of Southwest humor. Mark Twain, in the guise of what would otherwise be the Whig gentleman, inquires of garrulous old Simon Wheeler for information on one Rev. Leonidas W. Smiley. Actually, it is a hoax on Mark, because there is no such person, but the mention of "Smiley" sets Wheeler off on a long story about Jim Smiley, an intrepid bettor who had made large sums on his miraculous frog that could out-

[11] Franklin Walker, ed., *The Washoe Giant in San Francisco* (San Francisco. George Fields, 1938), p. 29.
[12] *Ibid.*, p. 42.

jump any other in the county. In the course of his long monologue, Wheeler reveals that Smiley, too, was hoaxed by a stranger who filled Smiley's frog with heavy quail-shot. Thus, as Lynn points out, Clemens has put both the frame narrator and the yokel at a disadvantage; the political character of the whole tradition is revealed in the names of Smiley's fighting dog and jumping frog, Andrew Jackson and Daniel Webster. We can almost see this piece as a virtuoso hoax on the tradition itself, except that Clemens referred to it later as "that villainous backwoods sketch."

In various pieces, we find him calming down in intensity of effect, relying on subtler apprehensions, and coming much closer to what is permanently interesting. The series of reports on spiritualist seances, grouped together as "wildcat religions," is surprisingly temperate and just in tone. He also keeps his firing-piece in order by corrosively nasty invective against the San Francisco police. The greatest evidence of increasing sophistication is the way Clemens varies his own roles, appearing more often in the capacities Addison and Steele exercised. Theater, literary style, morality, manners, and politics now come into his purlieu.

≪§ §≫

Thus Clemens' early concept of expression was conditioned by folk material, newspaper writing, and the needs of the lecture platform. Throughout his career his greatest concern for craftsmanship is displayed in "How To Tell a Story," and much of his style is based on what he learned from oral delivery as a lecturer and after-dinner speaker. He is diametrically opposed, temperamentally, to the conscious, dedicated artist of the type of Flaubert or James—or Proust or Joyce. His habitual method of work was to write feverishly at long sittings (sometimes turning out 200 manuscript pages a week) until his inspiration died. Then he would pigeonhole the manuscript; sometimes he took it up again when interest revived, or when he needed money. Generally, he wrote best in the summer when there were fewer social distractions. He often wrote a huge bulk of manuscript much larger than he knew he would need, and then culled it for the best parts. When he and Warner collaborated on *The Gilded Age,* Clemens, even before the final draft, threw away 300 manuscript pages, whereas Warner cancelled only 50. Throughout the composition, there was seldom any conscious control or pre-ordained end in view. And in such works as *Pudd'nhead Wilson* and *The American Claimant,* where he did have a scheme in mind, he was easily deflected in mid-course. Both times he finished with two separate stories where he had intended one; in the case of the former, he divided the two stories, but in the case of the latter, he did not.

There are other evidences of this nervously excited, careless method of composition, which was in itself often motivated by garishly non-artistic considerations. The proportion of enthusiastic beginnings to completed works is unusually high. Deadlines always crippled him completely. Here and there he betrays a production-line attitude in his minute calculations of the number of words turned out for a certain period. When pressed by circumstances, as in the latter part of *Life on the Mississippi* and *A Tramp Abroad,* he poached on the most nondescript source materials.

Many of these habits, including his concern over illustrations, are predicated on the conditions of subscription publishing. It proved such an inexhaustible gold mine in the case of *Innocents Abroad* that he organized the Webster Company on this plan. The arrangement called for a gaudily decorated, elephantine volume which agents sold in door-to-door solicitation long before the date of publication. The bigger and more impressive the volume, the better it sold in the provinces. Except *a posteriori* in the case of Clemens, the literary goods of subscription publishing were of no significance, and few "respectable" authors of Howells' sort would have anything to do with this plan.

He was attracted to subscription publishing because, unmistakably, writing for Clemens was at least in part a means of making more and more money. In a peak year, he made and spent $100,000. The whole atmosphere of literary Hartford solidly confirmed this drive, as Kenneth R. Andrews points out in *Nook Farm.* Protection of English and Canadian copyrights, advance serialization, and advance favorable reviews were all matters of top importance in Clemens' mind.

This whole method of composition had its advantages, aside from the fact that it was dictated by his temperament. It enabled him to compose spontaneously and colloquially, getting onto paper by the most direct method all the richness and dash of the born raconteur. His hot rages and implacable hatreds produced profanity which must have been a deeply gratifying aesthetic experience in its own right. His devoted servant Katy Leary says: ". . . his swearing never seemed really bad to me. It was sort of funny, and a part of him somehow. Sort of amusing it was—and gay—not like real swearing, 'cause he swore like an angel!" While the elaborate taboos of his age and environment exercised a restraint which we shall consider shortly, it is undoubtedly the undercurrent of this ornate and deeply creative profanity that wells onto his pages. It is in *informality* that Clemens hits his apogee. We are speaking here of the manner for which he is best known as a humorist and genial commentator. The two other major aspects of his style, the tense and heightened eloquence of many descriptive and melodramatic passages and the sentimentality that crops up here and there, have not borne up well with the passage of time. One suspects that they were good in their day, and even in an age such as ours, that values a Hemingway's corrosively aseptic style, such passages have their quaint appeal.

We can see that his informal method would be ideally suited to revealing the feel of things in the boom days of Mississippi River traffic and the frenzied and nightmarish quest for quick riches in the West. The eloquence and sentimentality, though, are formed in the molds of Victorian taste which he encountered in the East.

᠀᠍ ᠍

While Clemens' journalistic days spanned his Western period, we must remember that his first significant book was the result of a pleasure excursion of rich and middle-aged tourists who stopped at all the sacred shrines of European art and history and the Biblical lands. Here Clemens was involved on the fringes of solid Victorian culture, and the colloquial anecdote and humor of the frontier had to be adapted to more refined and cosmopolitan content. Thus we can appreciate his total achievement only by taking into account the influence both of the West and the East, and more particularly the points at which such influences overlapped.

The mining speculation in the West was simply another aspect of the Eastern robber-baron culture. For many more years than he spent on the frontier, Clemens was immersed in the padded luxuries, sumptuous dinners, and nouveau-riche crudities of post-Civil War America. His father-in-law was a famous entrepreneur in coal and lumber, and in Clemens' correspondence and his autobiography, we have glimpses of Mugwump politics, of monopoly business tactics, war in the Philippines, Grover Cleveland, Theodore Roosevelt, a case of Scotch whiskey from "St. Andrew" Carnegie, yachting expeditions with H. H. Rogers, and the like.

Certainly the focus of polite Eastern culture in his life was centered in his wife and in his deep friendship with William Dean Howells. Both of them represented, to him, the pinnacle of a refinement and a delicacy of apprehension that he instinctively knew he could never attain unaided, but which he longed for nevertheless. His long probation and testing as a possible son-in-law to the staid Langdons marked the crisis of the East-West dichotomy during his early maturity. The warm affection of Howells saw him through the many difficult narrows in Eastern society. He expressed his gratitude to Howells in the literary sphere too:

> And that reminds me—ungrateful dog that I am—that I owe as much to your training as the rude country job printer owes to the city boss who takes him in hand & teaches him the right way to handle his art. I was talking to Mrs. Clemens about this the other day & grieving because I had never mentioned it to you, thereby seeming to ignore it or be unaware of it. Nothing that has passed under your eye needs any revision before going into a volume, while all my other stuff does require so *much*.[13]

It is the inviolable sub-stratum of frontier gusto which we surveyed in this chapter that provides all the ingratiatingly uncombed and unbuttoned boyish traits, and it is the Eastern civilization that washes the face and straightens the tie.

৺ ৶

"Mark Twain," then, is an artificial artistic synthesis made up of a native tradition of humorous writing enriched and transformed by the personal characteristics of Samuel Clemens. As Twain's reputation grew, Clemens himself developed—largely through foreign travel, marriage, financial ventures, and a very busy social life. He carried into these new contexts a freshness, an abandon, and a highly ironic comic vision already associated in the public mind with the "Jumping Frog" sketch. Thus eventually the artistic construction came to seem more real than the real man.

This chapter has traced the beginnings of this development in newspaper writing and travel letters. The colloquialism of the language, the shortness of the composition, the joke structure of the anecdote, and the informality of tone became permanently identified with the wit that stemmed from his ironic commentaries. All these qualities have made the name "Mark Twain" congenial and beloved.

---

[13] Henry Nash Smith and William M. Gibson, eds., *Mark Twain–Howells Letters* (Cambridge. Massachusetts, The Belknap Press of Harvard University Press, 1960), p. 226.

❧ AUTOBIOGRAPHICAL WORKS

E VERY vital word that Clemens wrote is derived directly from personal experience. In this sense, all his works are in varying degrees autobiographical except *The Prince and the Pauper,* because as Howells remarks, "the scene being laid in England, in the early part of the sixteenth century, the difficulties presented to a nineteenth-century autobiographer were insurmountable." [1] But for the reader who attempts to see even Clemens' avowedly autobiographical work as literal transcription, the difficulties will be insurmountable.

The *Autobiography* itself gives us the closest view of Samuel Clemens the man, although it is marked by a desire to make experience interesting at any cost. *Roughing It* and *Life on the Mississippi,* by contrast, deal with Mark Twain, a somewhat artificial and conventionalized, but wise and scintillating personality that captured the devotion of the entire world. The reporting of fact is no more efficient in these two volumes, but since they are more frankly "artistic," the inaccuracies serve a creative function.

Of these three efforts, the conscious attempt at autobiography is not an unqualified literary success, whereas the more casually conceived early passages of the Mississippi book and the whole of *Roughing It* are among the most popular of his writings, peren-

[1] William Dean Howells, *My Mark Twain* (New York, Harper and Brothers, 1910), pp. 137–8.

37

nially delightful in their sweep of locale, their garish color, their humor, and the geniality of their humane sympathy. However, it will be best to begin with the direct reminiscences.

❧ ❧

Except for a few pieces written in the 70's and 90's, the bulk of the *Autobiography* was dictated in 1906–08, when Clemens was in his early 70's, a widower who whiled away many a morning hour in rambling reminiscence. Albert Bigelow Paine, his literary executor, published about half the manuscript material (a selection of over 700 pages) printed in order of composition, in 1924. In 1940 Bernard DeVoto, then custodian of the Mark Twain Papers, published about half the remaining papers, grouped around a series of relevant topics, under the title *Mark Twain in Eruption*. Finally, in 1959, Charles Neider made the inevitable attempt to redeem the book by editing a new version with the contents arranged in chronological order.

The principles which Clemens thought would guarantee success in autobiographical writing are:

> Start it at no particular time of your life; wander at your free will all over your life; talk only about the thing which interests you for the moment; drop it the minute its interest threatens to pale, and turn your talk upon the new and more interesting thing that has intruded itself into your mind meantime.[2]

He also respected another rule, given to his brother: "Keep in mind what I told you—when you recollect something which belonged in an earlier chapter, do not go back, but jam it in *where you are*. Discursiveness does not hurt an autobiography in the least." [3] He directly eschewed chronology for "a form and method whereby the past and the present are constantly brought face to face, resulting in contrasts which newly fire up the interest all along like contact of flint with steel." [4] Lastly, he prides himself on treating ordinary persons and undistinguished events.

The Paine volumes follow the author's intent in presenting the material in the random order in which it presented itself to Clem-

---

[2] *Mark Twain's Autobiography,* Stormfield Edition (New York, Harper and Brothers, 1929), Vol. 1, p. 193.
[3] Albert Bigelow Paine, ed., *Mark Twain's Letters* (New York, Harper and Brothers, 1911), p. 379.
[4] *Autobiography,* Vol. 2, p. 245.

ens' associative memory. Unfortunately, it is precisely this method which is at fault. Since it was dictated to a stenographer, the length of a passage is governed largely by the proportions of the spoken anecdote. Aside from this, it has little organization or procedure. It consists of character sketches, opinions, diary entries, letters, newspaper quotes, and reminiscences interlarded with passages from his daughter Susy's teen-age biography of her father.

The reader is immersed in the day-to-day workings of Clemens' mind, at the expense of plowing through long stretches of dull and trivial material, such as a garrulous exploration of a poorly furnished Florentine villa, including a description of every inch of fabric in room after room. In fact, some of the material could hardly have been included with any possible reader in mind; it represents an elderly man's desire to cling to and hoard up detail for the sake of detail; there could hardly be any other justification for recording Clemens' exasperated replies to an editor's grammatical and rhetorical corrections of a text which the reader never sees. Other material represents mistakes in judgment: when one of Theodore Roosevelt's secretaries denied a petitioner access to the President, and employed physical violence in the process, Clemens thought the scandal was symbolic of a degenerating democracy; he included long swatches of newspaper clippings about the incident, thinking it would have been justified by history at the time of publication, since he did not intend for some of the work to appear until one hundred years after his death.

What this book reveals of Clemens' life is uncertain. The looseness of fact is a compound of poor memory and of his unerring sense of which personal experiences make a good story and how the material ought to be managed in terms of timing, climax, and such tricks of audience control. Here, to be sure, he practices his art.

The discursiveness does pay off now and then with accidental felicities. For example, at one point he describes how Jim Wolfe crawled out on an icy roof to silence caterwauling cats, only to fall into the middle of a candy-making party in his nightshirt. This raucous comedy is immediately followed by a treatment of childhood nightmares and guilt obsessions.

In addition, some of the passages on his early experience rise to an exceptionally high level of lyric feeling, totally uncontaminated by the gaudy trappings of Victorian rhetoric that dangle like beads from many of the notable travel descriptions. Particularly in treating childhood days on his uncle's farm, he attains in prose a simple and genuine kind of poetry that one feels instinctively is what Whitman should have produced:

> I can call back the solemn twilight and mystery of the deep woods, the earthy smells, the faint odors of the wild flowers, the sheen of rain-washed foliage, the rattling clatter of drops when the wind shook the trees, the far-off hammering of woodpeckers and the muffled drumming of wood pheasants in the remoteness of the forest, the snapshot glimpses of disturbed wild creatures scurrying through the grass—I can call it all back and make it as real as it ever was, and as blessed.[5]

This passage continues at some length with a rhythmically insistent and lyrical catalogue of all the sights, sounds, and smells of a country boyhood.

Another masterful touch is the listing of village tragedies: the slave fatally knocked in the head with a chunk of slag, the young Californian emigrant stabbed by a drunken comrade, the group of ruffians trying to shoot their uncle with a gun that repeatedly fails, the drunken tramp burning in jail with matches unwittingly supplied by Sam, poor old Snarr shot down in the main street, and the lone widow and her daughter, shooting point-blank the bawdy, drunken, would-be attacker. Clemens recreates the lonely and hopeless night-time fears of a child who imagines that Providence is staging all these deaths simply to induce him to repent—and the blithe daytime forgettings. These memories are profoundly moving and have the note of authenticity that marks the best of the fiction drawn from these sources, notably *Tom Sawyer* and *Huckleberry Finn*.

The "third volume" of the autobiography, Bernard DeVoto's *Mark Twain in Eruption,* has a natural appeal since it consists largely of suppressed papers which Paine thought it inadvisable to make public in 1924. In addition, DeVoto's admirable method of arranging materials so that each section is addressed to one major topic vastly improves this volume in comparison with the earlier ones. The title suits it excellently, since the material consists of frank and devastating assessments (often distorted by rage) of contemporary public figures. Treatments of Theodore Roosevelt and Andrew Carnegie are followed by a series of pieces on "The Plutocracy," a group of corrupt and hypocritical politicians and business men. These are the days of Ida Tarbell and the Muckrakers, but Clemens presents his views of the "damned human

[5] *Ibid.,* Vol. I, p. 110.

race" with a different emphasis. He long felt that America was irresistibly drifting toward a monarchy. He supported this view by proofs from Roman history, by invidious interpretations of human character, and by invoking simple destiny. And he saw the plutocracy as hastening this end.

These pieces, along with "Two Halos," his publishing memoirs, are unexampled exercises in vituperation, mud-slinging, and downright nastiness that probably surpass anything produced by H. L. Mencken. Although one finds, here and there, a distinctly paranoid rancor against and suspicion of others, and a tendency toward vilification, Clemens is magnificent when his moral dander is up. Senator Clark of Montana, Jay Gould, Senator Simon Guggenheim of Colorado, John D. Rockefeller, Jr., John Wanamaker, and "the McCurdies, McCalls, Hydes, Alexanders, and the rest of that robber gang who have lately been driven out of their violated positions of trust in the colossal insurance companies of New York" are roasted, toasted, broiled, and baked. Here he shows the fury that Howells said underlay all his fun. But then he takes the sting out of these denunciations by an adulatory piece on the Rockefeller Institute.

"Hannibal Days" contains the valuable and interesting recollections of early attempts at prayer, of minstrel shows, and of a wonderful bout with a traveling mesmerizer. Sam presents himself as a boy impervious to hypnosis, who nevertheless covets the notoriety of becoming the most tractable and marvelous of the demonstrator's subjects. Whether or not he faked the whole series of "demonstrations," the chain of events, including the satisfaction of his vanity and his mother's refusal to believe that he was pretending all these reactions, is the typical dilemma which he repeatedly puts Mark Twain and Tom Sawyer through.

Charles Neider's edition of the *Autobiography* is an attempt to reshuffle this material in a chronological form. The new passages he adds are of slight importance, although he noticeably improves the book by his decision to exclude much verbiage that Paine gave dutiful place to. If it occasionally seems a pity that he has cut out so much of the crackling anger of the DeVoto book, this version is nonetheless the best one for the general reader, for whom Mr. Neider designated the volume. But DeVoto's idea of grouping material in relevant batches still makes *Mark Twain in Eruption* the most satisfyingly unified book of the three, the one that comes closest, among the avowedly autobiographical material, to what Mr. Neider claims for his—"a classic of American letters."

The human person behind these documents—Samuel Clemens himself—is distinct: a nervous, high-strung man, very sensitive to irritating noises, given to superlatives, sudden excitements, and hot rages. Sentimental about old friends and convivial times, he can also hold adamantine grudges like the one against Bret Harte. He has little intellectual subtlety or power, falling easily into such mental traps as the use of impressive statistics to back up whatever *idée-fixe* he has settled on. His inordinate vanity is revealed in name-dropping and the elaborately disguised quotation of compliments that are made the more obvious by the very effort to hide them. On the other hand, in his give-away protestations of ignorance, weakness, and fallibility, he disarms his critic in advance. His fierce crusading for probity in public life gives him a moral stature that is not appreciably lessened by the nearly hysterical tone that sometimes creeps in. It is a childlike but lovable bag of tricks—as if an Old Testament prophet had been crossed with a prima donna, a naughty little boy, and the village wiseacre.

In turning to the more specialized books of autobiography, *Roughing It* and *Life on the Mississippi,* we find many of the same characteristics revealed in mining and reportorial experiences and piloting days, but this time projected through the mask of Mark Twain.

⋞ ⋟

Roughing It (1872) came after *The Innocents Abroad* as the second of Clemens' significant books, thus appearing considerably earlier in his career than any of the other autobiographical material. It covers the period in his life from his abandonment of soldiering in 1861, through his experiences as a miner and reporter in Nevada, California, and Hawaii, to the highway-robbery hoax perpetrated on him by friends in 1866. Thus he is also writing about experiences closer in recollection to the actual writing than those drawn upon in any of the other autobiographical works.

Nevertheless, he had completely forgotten the stagecoach journey from St. Joseph, Missouri, to Carson City, Nevada, with which he intended to open the book, and had to write for the journal of the trip kept by his brother Orion, who, accompanied by Sam, was traveling west to assume the Territorial Secretaryship of Nevada. The first twenty chapters of the book recount this jolting, gruelling trip, with Sam, Orion, and Mr. Bemis stretched out on the bumpy mail sacks. The trek across the waste stretches of the continent is related in a peculiarly genial and mild tone, un-ruffled and rambling, in the manner of a true pipe-smoking ra-conteur. Here he is not straining to fill up pages, as he does to-ward the end of the Mississippi volume, and the chapters are much more coherent in tone. The digression on Slade, the reckless desperado of the Rockies (which resembles the account of Mu-rel's gang in *Life on the Mississippi*); the descriptions of alkali deserts, sagebrush, jackass rabbits and coyotes; and the account of the stagecoach and pony express organizations all take their place in the narrative. The only notable disruption of tone is in the sledge-hammer brutality of the humor in Chapter XV. Here he glories in Brigham Young's monumental and legendary diffi-culties in appeasing the jealousies of his polygamous household.

After the arrival in Carson City and the hilarious scene in Mrs. O'Flannigan's boarding-house-barracks the night the dozen pet tarantulas got loose, comes an idyllic interlude in which Twain and John Kinney make an unsuccessful attempt to establish a timber claim on scenic Lake Tahoe. The next two chapters, XXIV and XXV, could bear very detailed examination as two classic (and antithetic) instances of Twain's humor.

Chapter XXIV concerns his purchase of a genuine "Mexican plug," an intractably vicious bucking bronco. The bilking of the newly arrived immigrant, one of the most exhausted clichés of frontier humor, is here given a treatment that makes it perennially delightful. As in the case of the "Jumping Frog" yarn, Twain here carries one form of traditional humor to its apotheosis. Only in Faulkner's "Spotted Horses" does this horse-trading yarn meet its equal. One of the most skillful effects is the subdued econ-omy of ironic verbal effects. As Twain is sizing up the beast, "a man whom [he] did not know (he turned out to be the auc-tioneer's brother)" whispers " 'I know that horse—know him well. You are a stranger, I take it, and so you might think he was an American horse, maybe, but I assure you . . . he is, without the shadow of a doubt, a Genuine Mexican Plug!' " At the crucial moment when Twain is wavering in the purchase, he adds " 'He can out-buck anything in America!' " Twain shortly learns the truth of this statement by getting bruised, pummelled, and rup-tured in his attempt to stay on the volcanic animal. It is no lini-ment to his wounds to hear this from one "elderly-looking com-forter":

'Stranger, you've been taken in. Everybody in this camp knows that horse. Any child, any Injun, could have told you that he'd

43

buck; he is the very worst devil to buck on the continent of America. . . . And moreover, he is a simon-pure, out-and-out, genuine d—d Mexican plug, and an uncommon mean one at that, too. Why, you turnip, if you had laid low and kept dark, there's chances to buy an *American* horse for mighty little more than you paid for that bloody old foreign relic.'

It is only a highly disciplined kind of art that can evoke this sort of effect.

Chapter XXV discusses the distressing but hilarious difficulties of administering a raw and reckless territory on grants and regulations issued by a distant bureaucracy that adamantly refuses to recognize local variations in prices. Although Orion's honesty is never shaken when he is docked for each discrepancy between federal grants and local expenses, Mark Twain shows in his exasperation at his brother's high principles how insensibly a civil servant is tempted to become a polite pickpocket. The bronco incident is related in the intimately personal tone of the yarn-spinning tradition; the discussion of political administration has its personal aspects too, but its significance lies in its broad awareness of the moral complexity of government. In this it forecasts many a passage in *The Gilded Age*.

Chapter XXVI initiates the mining recollections with an account of a "prospecting party" to Humboldt. Disappointed here, he goes over to the Esmeralda area in a trip that is rich in humorous anecdotes: the overbearing bully, "Mr. Arkansas," being done in by the inn-keeper's wife as she brandishes her scissors under his nose; the escape from the flood; and the fearful repentances of Twain, Ballou, and Ollendorff before what appears to them to be certain death in a snow storm. At Esmeralda, the fascinating trip to alkaline Mono Lake and Twain's and Higbie's experiences as "millionaires for a week" are compelling stories, regardless of the degree of truth in them, that combine humor, adventure, danger, and awe, along with a lyric excitement about natural beauties.

Volume Two opens with Twain's becoming a reporter for the *Virginia City Territorial Enterprise*. The early chapters are rich in anecdotes of the flush times, with desperadoes, speculators, Indians, Chinese, "nabobs," and miners swarming through the pages. Just enough technical explanations of mining processes are given to satisfy the curiosity which the rest of the narration stimulates—which cannot quite be said for the cetology in *Moby Dick*.

Chapter XII relates the incomparably funny "story of the Old

Ram," the extremest form of the shaggy-dog tale in which the drunken Jim Blaine never does get around to speaking of the ram because of the seductive interest of all the lugubrious side issues. He is repeatedly distracted by Miss Wagner, who borrowed a disastrously ill-fitting glass eye, wooden leg, and wig from her variously decrepit cronies; Jacops, the intrepid coffin peddler who waited like a buzzard outside the house of sickness; Deacon Dunlap's son-in-law, the missionary who was boiled and eaten; and Uncle Lem, whose back was broken in two places when an Irishman carrying a hod of bricks fell on him.[6] This piece recalls the "cameo" treatment of the same effect in "The Celebrated Jumping Frog."

Chapters XIV and XVII present his recollections of his days as a California journalist, although most biographers agree that he is inaccurate in his account of leaving Virginia City for San Francisco, and quitting the San Francisco *Morning Call.*

Then, after a scant account of his second mining attempt (again ignoring the real cause of his flight from the city), he closes the book, beginning with Chapter XXI, with a description of his trip to the Sandwich Islands on the *Ajax,* as a correspondent for the Sacramento *Union.*

The character sketch of the "Old Admiral," a retired whaleman on board the *Ajax,* is one of the richest in Twain's repertoire. A heavy-drinking temperance advocate given to retailing horrendous lies about atrocities committed by Yankee ministers against Southern ladies, he meets his match in Williams, one of the passengers. Referring to the same secessionist newspaper which the Old Admiral uses as his authority, Williams manufactures even more blood-curdling Southern ministerial atrocities, throwing in a swollen-legged epileptic as a victim for good measure.

On arrival in the Islands, Twain indulges in that peculiar blend of subjects which we shall encounter in *Life on the Mississippi.* In what Edgar Marquess Branch calls "polymorphic composition," lyric apostrophes on scenery are followed by comically exaggerated complaints about the discomfort caused by insects, or by exhaustive accounts of the prices of horses and saddles. To be sure, this range of subjects may have been exactly calculated to satisfy his Sacramento newspaper readers. But in all this hectic hodge-

---

[6] Readers who are interested in the technical differences between a written and spoken passage in Clemens' style will find it rewarding to compare this tale with his transcription of the version he used in a lecture, given in *Mark Twain in Eruption,* pp. 217–28.

podge of conflicting interests, Twain seldom seems to see the nearly comic discrepancies between the spiritualized appreciation of scenery and the hard-headed calculation of the cost of shipping grain from San Francisco. Only rarely does he exploit these contrasts, as when Oahu, his stupid and lazy horse, sits down just as the rider reaches the apex of a poetic meditation.

It is difficult to assess the amount of skill that went into the account of Hawaii, since the material is in itself so fresh and interesting that one feels the chapters wrote themselves. The bloody history of the Islands and of Captain Cook's adventures, the food, the vegetation, the comic-opera government, and the scenery —all are blended into a fascinating account which gives us a hopeful foretaste of what we shall encounter in Twain's travel experiences. The highlights in these pages range from the familiar comic techniques through the high-pitched excitement of dangerous adventures, to the rapturous apostrophes on sunsets and rainbows.

Of these three departments, the comic is best represented by Chapter XXIX, a spoof of Horace Greeley's notoriously illegible handwriting. We meet a madman who had written to Horace Greeley for advice about how to cure a young farmer of an obsession to make turnip vines climb. The illegible reply from the editor of the *Tribune* is given in four ludicrous "translations" whose production must have contributed to the weakening of the correspondent's sanity.

Chapters XXXIII and XXXIV combine the picturesque and the adventurous in an account of the scenic wonders of the crater of Kilauea Volcano, first as seen from above, and later as it appears to two invincibly curious and foolhardy tourists (Twain and a stranger named Marlette) who traverse the floor of the crater on foot at night. They jump over deep fissures and white-hot lava and frequently lose their way, until Marlette falls through the weak crust up to his shoulders.

The book ends with a brief relation of Twain's return to San Francisco, and the beginning of his career as a lecturer, in which he capitalized on the Hawaiian experiences.

ക്ട ട്ര

Like many of Clemens' books, *Life on the Mississippi* had a complex genesis. Begun as a series of articles for Howells' *Atlantic Monthly* (January to June and August, 1875) and finally completed as a book in 1882–3, it comprises his legacy of river lore.

The "Baton Rouge"

47

Incontestably, Chapters IV through XVII (the *Atlantic* portion), and XVIII through XX represent a choice tapping of Clemens' creative memory, when the sap was running high. But as he says himself, ". . . emotions are among the toughest things in the world to manufacture out of whole cloth; it is easier to manufacture seven facts than one emotion." Chapters I through III, a pastiche of historical and statistical material, interlarded with quotations from Parkman, are a sorry proof that too often in the flurry of filling out an impressive volume for subscription purposes, he contented himself with the seven facts rather than waiting and working for the one emotion.

Chapters IV through XX are clearly and consecutively organized on the progressive difficulties of learning to pilot a large steamboat through the intricate and constantly shifting channels of the "twelve or thirteen hundred miles" of river from St. Louis to New Orleans. Within this overall structure, anecdotes, facts, and humor find a flawless natural expression. The style and rhetoric, admirable as they are, do their work unobtrusively. In all, it is a leading example of the best kind of informal, unconscious artistry, and for these pages alone, Clemens deserves a high rank.

In his account in the autobiography of his apprenticeship as a printer, we learn a fair amount about the living conditions in the household of his employer, Joseph P. Ament, and about how the boy spent his leisure; but in the story of his apprenticeship to the pilot Horace Bixby, we have a classic account of the brash youth up against the complex exigencies of adult work, supervised by a proud and profane master. Learning all the "points" along the river, and their changing shapes in various conditions of light and dark, is only the beginning of this bewildering discipline which also requires that he know the shifting depths of the river at multifarious points, and how to read the deceptive surface of the water for what lies underneath. Although Clemens had not originally planned to devote the entire *Atlantic* series to piloting, the subject seemed to assert itself and expand under his hands as he worked, so that it provided the structural foundation out of which grew all the rich comedy and humane wisdom of this account.

Chapters LIII through LVI, comprising his visit to boyhood haunts, are a valuable supplement to the Hannibal passages in the *Autobiography* and *Mark Twain in Eruption*. We saw in Chapter I that Clemens retained intact the atmosphere of his boyhood, and all the adult intellectual fulminations remained but variations on the Calvinist dilemmas of childhood. This is demonstrated again in the brilliant presentation in Chapters LIV and LVI of the same theme. Terrifying thunderstorms are sent to warn the young boy that he will die as swiftly as Lem Hackett, a notorious sinner, if he does not mend his ways. As he lies abed, he cunningly produces prayers which "accidentally" enumerate all the sins of his playmates, in the hope that God will take them first. Then the rest of the night is passed in even profounder guilt, for having endangered these playmates. This self-intensifying and self-defeating round of guilt convictions is even more powerfully and sensitively evoked in the bedroom interview with his brother Henry. The latter assures him that the boy (actually Sam himself) who gave the drunken tramp the matches with which he burnt himself to death in the jail is actually a murderer. These passages have the appeal of finely-sensed psychological analysis, of drama, and of truth.

At Chapter XXI, he commits a colossal *non sequitur* by jumping ahead to 1882 and a detailed account of his adult and disillusioned view of the river when the whole glorious rush of steamboat traffic had all but disappeared and even in handling the flush days, as DeVoto and others have pointed out, he filters out all the prostitution, and most of the gambling and other crudities and shoddinesses of the period. The whole book, then, is a kind of autumnal afterglow of a bawdy and blustering era.

Here the over-all structure is a loose account of a trip south from St. Louis to New Orleans, and north again to Minneapolis–St. Paul. He digresses into statistics on local commerce, detailed grammatical analysis, the economics of cotton planting, controversies over the Army Corps of Engineers' program of river improvement, and countless other vaguely related topics. He stops the narrative for long and blissfully irrelevant yarns. And he gives exhaustive technical accounts of changes in river topography that could only interest professional pilots.

Clemens' sojourn in New Orleans provided interesting, if perfunctorily presented, glimpses of a cock-fight, a mule race, and a visit with G. W. Cable and J. C. Harris. The most notable aspect of this section of the book is the hotly argued theory that Sir Walter Scott was the source of a romanticism that proved destructive to Southern culture. Although it could hardly stand the test of modern "scientific" sociology, the theory is presented convincingly, with the medieval turrets of the Old Capitol at Baton Rouge standing as the symbol of a degenerate state of mind.

The book peters out in an account of a trip from St. Louis

north, thick with statistics and panegyrics to the pushy commer-
cialism and thriving materialism of the upper river.

Some of the most interesting materials, from a literary point of
view, are the yarns. At the crudest level is the tale whose pattern
has a kind of stone-age subtlety. It is the "O. Henry" pattern
that reserves one important fact or circumstance which, when
revealed at the end, bowls over the whole set of expectations
laboriously cultivated in the reader's mind. Its derivation from
lecture-platform technique should be obvious. Thus "The Professor's Yarn" of Chapter XXXVI works up our sympathies for
a naive Ohio cattle man who will certainly lose $10,000 to profes-
sional gamblers. At the last minute, Clemens reveals to the reader
that the cattle man is a gambler in disguise who fleeces his
would-be fleecers. The same pattern, much more complexly
worked out, is seen in the "Karl Ritter" tale of Chapter XXXI,
blended with motifs of revenge, detective ratiocination, and terror
in the Poe vein. In the death watch scenes—where a roomful of
corpses lie, each with a string on his thumb attached to a bell
in case he has suffered a trance rather than death—we encounter
another indication of Clemens' deep-seated preoccupation with
the more lurid aspects of death and putrefaction. Later he indulges
this interest to the hilt in his treatment of New Orleans ceme-
teries and undertakers.

For the rest, the yarns are largely to be classified by subject
matter. We can note the "tall tale," as in the feats of Louisiana
mosquitoes in Chapter XXXIV, and the "deceiving the yokel"
variety in Chapters XXX and XXXIV. In both the latter cases,
however, the "yokel" is Clemens himself who knows more about
piloting than his lying informant, but who encourages the man in
order to see how far he will go with his ridiculous alligator stories.
When Clemens exposes the impostor, we have a combination,
then, of the "O. Henry" and "tall tale" varieties. Thus Clemens
continues, as he did in the "Jumping Frog" story, to use the
spare artistic materials provided by tradition in a rather complex
manner.

It must be recognized that there is a difference in Twain between the "tall tale" and the "yarn" drawn from personal experience. An example of the latter is the account in Chapter III of a
bogus letter from a newly converted and pious convict which,
read from innumerable pulpits, had evoked universal weeping.
Throughout the account Clemens again allows the reader to suppose the letter to be genuine; only at the end does he reveal the

imposture. Thus the form which he undoubtedly developed to handle legendary material is applied to actual experience. On the other hand, the opposite technique occurs as well; in the Karl Ritter tale, for example, manifestly nonsense from the beginning, he doggedly presents all kinds of circumstantial detail to convince the reader that the events actually took place. The result is that no matter whether an account is legendary material supported circumstantially or actual experience elaborated with legend, it is always drawn from the never-never land between fact and fiction, the region presided over by Twain's inimitable genius. And despite limitations, such as the crude attempt to use Indian legends for comic effects, his superlative handling of folk materials is a form of genius.

Life on the Mississippi is also notable because it was composed at the same time Clemens was working on *Huckleberry Finn,* and the material of the two books is so close that overlapping would have been unavoidable. Chapter III, in fact, was written for Huck, but inserted in this volume unchanged. As an account of the kind of courtly profanity of the bargemen, it is invaluable to this book in working up atmosphere. The details of the feuds as described in Chapter XXVI parallel material in the Shepherdson-Grangerford melee in Huck, and Chapters XXXVIII and LI deal with the "House Beautiful" and the "Richard III swordfight" that were to be mentioned in the novel.

The book takes on new interest as an autobiographical document in light of a recent emphasis by most leading critics on Clemens' rejection of the South and disgust with the river culture as expressed in *Huckleberry Finn.* It is said that the return to the river that was occasioned by the preparation of this book led Clemens to see his boyhood and adolescent memories in a new light. The beginning of this change in attitude is especially interesting if one reads the material in the 1944 edition of Edward Wagenknecht, which presents "suppressed" portions of *Life on the Mississippi* in which Clemens has his say on various aspects of Southern mob psychology and in which he supports the disgusted reactions of early European travelers like Mrs. Trollope.

~§ §~

Ironically enough, Clemens' best writing about himself is contained in *Roughing It,* the volume in which he was least conscious of attempting personal reminiscence. In keeping his eye focused on Western culture, silver mining, and local color, he insensibly included a heartening and endearing portrait of his own personality.

Similarly in the first twenty chapters of *Life on the Mississippi,* where he strives to survey the typical experience of a river pilot, his own nature beams winningly between the lines.

But when he deliberately addressed himself to dredging up memories—as in the latter portions of *Life on the Mississippi* and in the *Autobiography*—the effect is labored and artificial, except for the childhood reminiscences of the *Autobiography*.

The three books taken together show contrasts that are illuminating even though accidental—the reader moves from the youthful dash of *Roughing It* to the querulous fussiness of age in the disjointed *Autobiography*. The precious passages on childhood memories in the latter, however, are pervaded by a gently lyrical tone that can only be attained by a man who knows the intensity of the disillusionment that can intervene between youth and age.

4

⋞§ TRAVEL

I N THE autobiographical volumes, we saw Mark Twain in a native context; as we follow him abroad, we find in his reactions to European and Middle Eastern culture an attitude remarkably different from those of Henry Adams and Henry James, two distinguished contemporaries who were also engaged, somewhat more self-consciously than Twain, in the endlessly fascinating game of comparing civilizations. Twain brings considerably less culture with him than many another traveler, and he is less disposed to absorb with ready sympathy the charm of a foreign atmosphere. But he has the energy and zest of the born tourist; he wants to see everything there is to see and he manages to cover most of the ground. Unlike many tourists, however, he refuses to be taken in by guides, and he refuses to admire everything he is told to simply because he is told to; he judges each new experience independently for its own inherent value. Although his family and traveling companions took their culture with a heavy seriousness, and he happily escorted his womenfolk to Bayreuth, he says that hearing a Wagnerian opera affected him like a toothache in the pit of his stomach, or like being slowly skinned alive.

Moreover, he and his family spent a great part of their life in transit. It all began as a means of producing interesting newspaper letters; then his first successful lecture was based on the Hawaiian travel. With the success of *The Innocents Abroad,* he had confirmed a pattern which culminated in his round-the-world tour of

1895–6, undertaken in order both to lecture and to collect material for a book. Thus travel was an inherent part of his way of life, and prolonged periods of residence abroad contributed substantially to his international reputation, especially in Germany.

On the whole, he was happiest in Germany, Switzerland, Austria, and England; throughout his life he retained a strong animosity toward the French and all their ways, and the Catholic Church was far too much in evidence for him ever to relax in Italy. He was certainly fond of cleanliness and order and the rather firm public moral code of "Anglo-Saxon" nations.

In the political, social, and economic sphere, we find him moving from an early qualified endorsement of the missionaries in Hawaii to the fiery denunciations against them and against all forms of imperialism and monarchy in his old age.

Unlike Henry James, Twain never did feel at home in Europe, despite years of residence abroad; there always creeps into his thought a longing for the familiar foods and heating arrangements of his native country. Even after he had attained enough of a working knowledge of German to permit attempts at translating poetry, he continued to regard the language with a comically exaggerated hostility that produced some of his finest international humor. In short, he retained to the end the legendary Missouri skepticism—"you've got to show me"—a loyalty to his own impressions that is admirably honest.

꧁ ꧂

The Hawaiian chapters of *Roughing It* utilized about one third of the letters Twain wrote for the Sacramento *Union* between March and June, 1866.[1] The material he did not use in the book may have been rejected simply for lack of space, but some of the cruder examples of humor may have been discarded on the grounds of taste; for Twain certainly had in mind a distinction between what was fit for a newspaper audience as opposed to a book audience, as we shall see in his revision of journalistic letters for *The Innocents Abroad*. Typical of the newspaper humor is a labored passage in which the wife of a whaling captain describes a street collision in nautical terms, which are then painfully annotated by Twain. Although other forms of parody were to find their way into later books, he thought it sage to omit two of his

---

[1] G. Ezra Dane, ed., *Letters from the Sandwich Islands* (Stanford University, California, Stanford University Press, 1938).

anti-romantic productions of the letters—a rhymed version of Polonius' advice to Laertes, and the other a poem composed of alternate lines from "The Destruction of Sennacherib" and "The Burial of Sir John Moore."

The letters also contain exhilarating flashes of anger, particularly when Twain speaks of his two archenemies, Mr. Harris, Minister of Finance and Attorney-General for the Hawaiian government and Bishop Staley of the Royal Hawaiian Established Reformed Catholic Church. His treatment of the Hawaiian Legislature is as violent, and as delightful, as his accounts of similar shenanigans on a grander scale in the Washington of *The Gilded Age*. Mark Twain seems to have formed his permanent opinion of legislators early in his Nevada experience as a parliamentary reporter; he remarked that the chaplain should not be fired as an unnecessary expense, since the legislator who had suggested the economy was most in need of ministration—he kept his feet on the desk and munched turnips during the morning prayer!

For the ordinary reader, the chapters in *Roughing It* give a sufficient—and exciting—view of his sojourn in the Sandwich Islands, although for tracing an author's mind at work, the comparison of the letters with the book is instructive.

☙ ❧

The twenty-six letters Twain wrote between December, 1866, and June, 1867, for the *Alta California,* are interesting primarily because they give us Twain's first detailed reaction to the East, aside from the smattering of letters written during his journeyman printer days in New York and Philadelphia.

He described his trip by steamer via the Isthmus of Nicaragua from California to New York, and his sojourn there, punctuated by a visit to his family that took him to St. Louis, Hannibal, Quincy, and Keokuk.[2] On the trip to New York, we find him settling into what was to be his famous manner. Commercial statistics, character sketches of passengers, descriptions of monkeys and parrots and the vegetation of the Isthmus, and assorted yarns told by captains and passengers—all these are on the familiar bill of fare. Some of these yarns are particularly interesting from a literary-historical point of view, because it was on this voyage that Twain first met Captain Ned Wakeman, whose figure was to haunt

[2] Franklin Walker and G. Ezra Dane, eds., *Mark Twain's Travels with Mr. Brown* (New York, Alfred Knopf, 1940).

many a later book, up to *Captain Stormfield's Visit to Heaven* of 1909. The great surprise of the trip is the calmness with which one of such an excitable nature takes a severe outbreak of cholera on the ship.

New York seems to offer so much distraction in itself that Twain's vulgar traveling companion, Mr. Brown, who appeared regularly during the voyage, all but retires, as Twain comments with increased subtlety and finesse on transportation, girlie shows, Russian baths, prices, popular preachers and churches, and his preparations for the *Quaker City* excursion. One of the most interesting sidelights of these letters is the obvious sophistication of the writer, even though he tends to measure most of what he sees against Pacific Coast standards. The interview with the President of the S. P. C. A. and the leader of the Midnight Mission (gentlemen who attempt to reform prostitutes) could appear in the *New Yorker* today with few changes. His attacks on the public vogue for the performances of Adelaide Ristori in Italian recall *Spectator* pieces against Italian opera, as do some of his other theatrical pieces. Not that he has lost any of the old frontier gusto. He can still make a great deal of the corpses of cholera victims left unburied in St. Louis, or guffaw over a Mrs. Mills' Mammarial Balm and Bust Elevator establishment in New York.

He carries a running comment on news items, some of them of historic import, such as Horace Greeley's bailing Jefferson Davis out of jail. He does devote much more attention to a famous brutal murder of the day—here we can see where he formed the habit that led to the inclusion of so much ephemeral trivia in his *Autobiography*.

All in all, he presents a fascinating and absorbingly detailed picture of New York in the days following the Civil War—bootblacks, drunken wastrels in police court, a new iron footbridge across Broadway, art exhibits, women's fashions, the offices of the American Bible Society, and drunken temperance picnics. In quality, these letters surpass anything he has hitherto produced for newspapers. Toward the end of the series, we find him, in Letter XXV, essaying a relatively new tone of seriousness mixed with distinct pathos in evoking the sense of crowded loneliness of the stranger in the big city.

෴

We have seen that in terms of his development, Clemens became progressively less and less provincial, but that the sphere of his audience increased in a widening proportion that was always slightly in advance of his sophistication. In this sense, *The Innocents Abroad* is an apt title. Not only is Mark Twain a very far cry indeed from Thomas Jefferson Snodgrass, he now has as his purlieu all of European, ancient, and Middle Eastern culture, instead of a steam engine going from St. Louis to Cincinnati.

The account of the voyage, which extended from June to November, 1867, is far enough removed from the present to begin to interest the modern reader as a kind of "period piece," a document in the intellectual and emotional drift and the unspoken tastes of the days following the Civil War. In itself, the trip was one of the first of the planned pleasure cruises, and represents a cultural milestone in the creative use of American leisure. But we find that the pious earnestness of the frequent prayer meetings and the reverent explorations of the Holy Land do not quite conform to modern ideas of leisurely relaxation—nor to Mark Twain's ideas. Yet we cannot call him modern when we observe his genuine discomfiture at seeing women expose their calves in a riotous can-can.

After the flurry of departure, dampened by bad weather and an enforced wait within the harbor, Twain smirks over the seasickness of the other passengers. Indeed, the opening of this book follows the formula of the Sandwich Island letters closely, although the stylistic finesse is much greater. The stop at the Azores gives Twain the first occasion for his condescending chauvinism when he boasts how one of our "turreted monitors" could blast the puny fort of Horta to bits.

Although the French remain one of his enduring exasperations in later years, he is excited by their rationality and neatness and precision, and is thoroughly won over by Napoleon III's revamping of Paris. Aside from the increasingly skillful manner in which he handles stock comic situations like the first visit to a French barber, the wretchedness of European billiard appointments, and Parisian guides, we can see a real literary achievement in his masterful command of the dichotomy as a means of organizing contrasting impressions. This is evident in the latter part of Chapter XIII when he contrasts Napoleon III and Abdul Aziz, Sultan of Turkey, or in Chapter XVI when he passes from the dazzling beauties of Versailles (which, in his childlike wonder, he very seriously compares to the Garden of Eden), to the tawdry, dark windings of the Faubourg St. Antoine. These passages are the first signs of a mature style.

One of the surest marks of this book as a "period piece" is what one might term the "Victorian" high style. This is a complex of characteristics combining an attitude of awe or of pious moralizing, along with a heightened, pompous diction, long stretches of euphuistic parallelism, and a fair sprinkling of exclamatory outbursts, embellished by saccharine imagery. It is almost impossible to decide, at this date, whether the clichés that also stud these passages were in any degree fresh in his day, although one does not seem to remember encountering them on the pages of other contemporary major authors. A good example in miniature is this apostrophe to the Milan Cathedral:

> What a wonder it is! So grand, so solemn, so vast! And yet so delicate, so airy, so graceful! A very world of solid weight, and yet it seems in the soft moonlight only a fairy delusion of frostwork that might vanish with a breath! How sharply its pinnacled angles and its wilderness of spires were cut against the sky, and how richly their shadows fell upon its snowy roof! It was a vision!—a miracle!—an anthem sung in stone, a poem wrought in marble!

His rapture over this ornate cathedral, and over the garishly *nouveau-riche* commemorative sculpture in the cemetery at Genoa, is part of his whole reaction to the "Old Masters." He is obviously conscious of his lack of artistic training and of his failure to appreciate such works as Leonardo's "Last Supper," over which his fellow tourists gush with emotion while he is manfully honest to his own feelings. In the first place, the "Last Supper" is so scaled and marred as to be nearly invisible. How can the others rhapsodize over the grace of gesture and the sublimity of expression in bodies and faces when all that is evident is a mildewed wall with scraps of color here and there? Twain is also exasperated with the predominately Roman Catholic content of the pictures, with the monotonously conventional poses, and with the representational inaccuracy that he repeatedly finds in these painters. Even more importantly, he becomes infuriated at the patronage system that produced this art; his bitter attack on the Medici Chapel of San Lorenzo in Florence is a classic indictment of the overbearing egotism of robber barons who have themselves painted in a group portrait with the Virgin and Saints. He expresses positive appreciation for the realistic Renaissance portraits and for Pompeiian bronzes, mosaics, and frescoes. His tongue-in-cheek raptures over a Venetian historical painting by Bassano is a masterpiece of burlesque art criticism.

Traveling southward through Italy, he cannot resist comparing Lake Como with Tahoe as he will also Galilee. In Chapter XXI he relates a burlesque crusaders' legend with the same relish that he showed in destroying the lush sentiment of the story of Heloise and Abelard when he visited Père la Chaise in Paris. He later gives the same treatment to the Seven Sleepers of Ephesus.

One of the most forceful parts of this volume is certainly Chapter XXV, in which the blunt and outspoken American materialist gives his views on the riches of the church in a land where beggars are ubiquitous. His admiration for efficient railroads and smooth highways and the supposedly firm financial health of Napoleon III's France—this whole constellation of ideas is part of the "period piece" too, since it is the standard attitude of the businessman era. These are the kinds of reforms that we shall see his Connecticut Yankee introducing into Arthurian England. He has not yet developed the convictions that issued in the "Plutocracy" attacks of *Mark Twain in Eruption*, where he saw that the American robber barons were only a few steps removed, in the temporal sphere, from the assumptions he makes about the princes of the church. And his suppressed exasperation at the apparent filth, laziness, and worthlessness of the inhabitants of Civita Vecchia is a familiar American stance, although his fairly frequent satiric treatment of American tourist shortcomings will endear him to any reader who has ever ventured out of the country. This is a mild sample: ". . . those old connoisseurs from the wilds of New Jersey who laboriously learn the difference between a fresco and a fire-plug, and from that day forward feel privileged to void their critical bathos on painting, sculpture, and architecture forevermore."

Before the volume is out, Twain gives away to buffoonery in treating the coliseum games, but Chapter XXVI, with its amusing description of America as it would appear to a peasant from Campagna, redeems matters. And the following one, with its clever advice for keeping one up on the guide, anticipates the technique of the modern British humorist, Stephen Potter.

Although limitations of space prevent detailed analysis, the second volume bristles with opinionated, sharply drawn impressions—the streets of Naples, the crater of Vesuvius, the ruins of Pompeii, and the Acropolis on a forbidden excursion by moonlight. After Constantinople, where his sympathy wears thin, interest picks up at Sebastopol, still in ruins from the Crimean War. At Odessa he makes his first visit to royalty, Czar Alexander II.

Ephesus and Smyrna lead to the overland trip from Beirut to Baalbeck and Damascus.

One senses a flagging of his energies here and there as the book proceeds, particularly when he employs some of the tricks of quotation and paraphrase that he used to pad out *Life on the Mississippi,* but his interest revives when he reaches the Holy Land. We know that later he was not inclined to credit the Bible with divine inspiration, but he maintains a tone of sweet reverence for the convictions of others that strikingly recalls some of the most winning qualities in his love letters. There is an almost feminine delicacy of feeling in his effort to accommodate himself to the wishes of others. But where the sensibilities of Protestant readers are not involved, he is merciless in his attacks on the relics of Catholic Europe.

The dirt, heat, flies, the cripples and beggars, wore his patience quite thin, and his exasperation at these rigors of camp life issues in an involved attack on Holy Land guide books. He cannot understand how former travelers found the area to be different from what it is—barren, rocky, desolate, and uncomfortable. This is the same perplexity he felt before the "Last Supper." Twain's anti-sentimentalism, which reaches its apogee in the Shepherdson-Grangerford chapters of *Huckleberry Finn,* comes to the fore in his satirizing one travel-writer's tear-burst which greeted each spot of sacred history. The copious grief occasioned by the tomb of Twain's distant ancestor, Adam, became one of the most famous passages from the book. As he approaches the Church of the Holy Sepulchre, the bludgeoning irony that was earlier applied to fragments of the True Cross in Europe tones down considerably, but there is still a strong undercurrent of doubt about the specific accuracy of the guides' assertions.

On the whole, he seems to have earned the animosity of his fellow passengers by the public expression of opinions like this: "Such was our daily life on board the ship—solemnity, decorum, dinner, dominoes, devotions, slander. It was not lively enough for a pleasure trip; but if we had only had a corpse it would have made a noble funeral excursion."

The newspaper letters, from which *The Innocents Abroad* grew, have only recently been published. In these the curious reader will find an insight into the deletions of vulgarity and plain speaking that he made, and into the literary revisions he found necessary.[3]

---

[3] Daniel Morely McKeithan, ed., *Traveling with the Innocents Abroad* (Norman, Oklahoma, University of Oklahoma Press, 1958).

None of the later travel accounts measure up to *The Innocents Abroad*. A. B. Paine, his biographer, and other critics give a large number of reasons for this decline—the pressure of deadlines, his wife's health, his increasing pessimism, and other such causes. However this may be, in these works there is a failure in the boyish bounce and freshness of reaction that characterize the account of the first European trip; there is a more obvious reliance on printed sources; and in the long anecdotes, there is a straining for effect— albeit with the best style and the most highly developed comic sense in the business.

❧ ☙

During 1878–9, about ten years after the publication of *The Innocents Abroad*, Mark Twain took an extended tour of Europe. In the meantime, he had intended writing a travel book about England, but the hospitality extended him during his visits in 1872–4 disarmed him. He knew by now that the formula for his kind of travel book had crystallized: the subscription trade called for a long volume, and his own interests and style led him to pro- duce a mélange of facts, history, curious personalities, and rather elaborate humorous stories. He knew too that his kind of humor was certain to offend many Englishmen, and he probably felt that the personal tone he had developed would force him to involve many a host in the anecdotes. Consequently, it was the trip to Germany, consciously undertaken for the purpose of writing a book, that produced *A Tramp Abroad* (1880).

There is clear evidence that Clemens did not want to write this book. When he lost the Swiss notebook, he rejoiced at being spared that part of the task, only to be forced to settle back to the job in gloom when the notebook showed up again. He appears simply to have been in permanent bad humor during the composition, as he remarks to Howells:

> I wish I *could* give those sharp satires on European life which you mention, but of course a man can't write successful satire except he be in a calm judicial good-humor—whereas I *hate* travel, & I *hate* hotels, & I *hate* the opera, & I *hate* the Old Masters—in truth I don't ever seem to be in a good enough humor with ANY– thing to *satirize* it; no, I want to stand up before it & *curse* it, & foam at the mouth,—or take a club & pound it to rags & pulp.[4]

4 Henry Nash Smith and William M. Gibson, eds., *Mark Twain–Howells Letters* (Cambridge, Massachusetts, The Belknap Press of Harvard University Press, 1960), pp. 248–9.

In Chapters II and III, Mark Twain, on a stroll in the woods near Heidelberg, is offended by the raucous attentions of the ravens, who seem to be commenting on his dress. This recalls to his mind the famous blue-jay yarn of Jim Baker, a frontier anecdote which he reproduces in the incomparable colloquial idiom of the "Jumping Frog." The point of the story, which depends more on manner than on matter, is the resemblance of these birds to human beings, as in the best of Aesop and La Fontaine; and while the story does not capitalize on the marital comedy of Chaucer's "Nun's Priest's Tale," it is as sure in its ironic effects. The jay that tries to fill a knot-hole in the roof with acorns calls in all the birds for miles around to exclaim at the wonder. After they have all been taken in by the prodigious hole, one of their number discovers it is in reality a house. The laughter and derision of the very birds that have been gulled is embarrassingly human.

The account of student duelling at Heidelberg (Chapters V–VII) is superior journalism heightened by a burlesque of the delicacies and niceties of the French duelling code in the subsequent chapter. Descriptions of Wagnerian opera and a German performance of "King Lear" are followed by an account of a trip down the Neckar by log raft and a hike in the Black Forest, heavily interlarded with legends, random diary entries, a thrust at ceramic collectors, and humorous drawings. After two interpolated American tales—"Nicodemus Dodge and the Skelton" and "The Man Who Put Up at Gadsby's"—Volume I closes with a Swiss interlude and the ascent of Rigi-Kulm, near Lucerne, where Twain and his traveling companion, Mr. Harris, fail twice, through their own comic ineptitude, to catch the scenic sunrise.

The character of the narrator continues to be the Mark Twain we met in the autobiographical books—in his chronic incompetence, he wrecks a raft of logs on the Neckar, and his nervous irritability is exercised by an epic attempt to find a sock in a dark bedroom without awakening his companion. The fraudulent effort to purchase a certificate proving he had climbed Mount Blanc adds to his laurels as a prevaricator.

The most elaborate performances of Volume II are a garrulous report of one of Harris's jaunts, sprinkled with distressing numbers of foreign terms, and a mock heroic ascent of a very minor peak, for which the terrified Twain provides himself with over 150 guides and servants and tons of supplies. The narration continues with technical information about glaciers (which parallels the piloting lore in *Life on the Mississippi* and the techniques of mining in *Roughing It*), copious cribbing from accounts of Alpine disasters, and a hurried treatment of northern Italy. Chapter XXI presents interesting evidence that Clemens was acutely aware of the double moral standard obtaining between painting and literature, and the psychological forces underlying this situation in his day. He quite rightly maintains that a verbal description of the pose of Titian's "Venus" would arouse furious indignation, whereas the painting is constantly on public view. It is a signal mark of Clemens' character that he should satisfy himself with complaint alone, rather than brave, as Joyce and Lawrence were to do later, the storm of bourgeois disapproval for trying to break this standard. It is also indicative of the tone of his age, too, which hardly encouraged such moral crusading.

Europe and Elsewhere is a selection of various travel letters and articles, many of which concern this same trip. Incidentally, these pieces point up his need to deal in earth-shaking superlatives. In "Marienbad—A Health Factory" he damns the German porcelain stove to the lowest reaches of hell for its complete failure to heat; in "Some National Stupidities" he praises the same stove just as inordinately as one of the greatest contrivances for human comfort.

※

Following the Equator, the last of his great travel books, was produced under the most inauspicious circumstances. The trip itself, we remember, was unwillingly undertaken as a round-the-world lecture tour to liquidate debts attendant on the failure of business enterprises. The voyage was punctuated by various ills, culminating in the news of the death of Susy Clemens when the family arrived in England. But when the book appeared in 1897, it proved smoother in tone than, and thus quite superior to, *A Tramp Abroad*, even if it does not approach the earlier books.

In this case, the exotic locales of Australia (Volume I) and India (Volume II) contribute an excitement that recalls the Nevada silver mines, Hawaii, and Europe when it was fresh to the young author. The contrast between this volume and *A Tramp Abroad* can also be seen in small details. In the Black Forest trip of the earlier book, Twain burlesques a typical Black Forest novel in a hectically vulgar account of a young girl's set of suitors, each of whom is judged by the magnitude of his manure pile (an account which apparently escaped both Howells and Olivia). In *Following the Equator*, the spoofing of the Australian "scrub" novel is far more just and equable.

The materials are familiar ones—commercial statistics and other measurements indulged in simply for the love of figures; tall tales; sketches of queer travelers and natives; scenic descriptions; catalogues of flora, fauna, and climate; and reforming diatribes. This last category becomes especially more prominent: the Queensland labor recruiting of Kanakas is brilliantly indicted as slavery and roundly denounced as only Twain could do it. He reaches a new peak of stately and measured, but burning hot, philippic in his ironic praise in Chapter XXI of the white man who poisoned a large group of aborigines by putting arsenic in a Christmas pudding:

> In many countries we have chained the savage and starved him to death; and this we do not care for, because custom has inured us to it; yet a quick death by poison is loving-kindness to it. In many countries we have burned the savage at the stake; and this we do not care for, because custom has inured us to it; yet a quick death is loving-kindness to it. In more than one country we have hunted the savage and his little children and their mother with dogs and guns through the woods and swamps for an afternoon's sport, and filled the region with happy laughter over their sprawling and stumbling flight, and their wild supplications for mercy; but this method we do not mind, because custom has inured us to it; yet a quick death by poison is loving-kindness to it. In many countries we have taken the savage's land from him, and made him our slave, and lashed him every day, and broken his pride, and made death his only friend, and overworked him till he dropped in his tracks; and this we do not care for, because custom has inured us to it; yet a quick death by poison is loving-kindness to it. In the Matabeleland to-day—why, there we are confining ourselves to sanctified custom, we Rhodes-Beit millionaires in South Africa and Dukes in London; and nobody cares, and all we ask is that no notice-inviting new ones shall be intruded upon the attention of our comfortable consciences.

This same sympathy extends to the Tasmanian natives in their war with the white settlers and to the Maoris in New Zealand; in these chapters, Twain shows a tender sympathy for the persecuted and bewildered savage, and a strong animus against the ignorant and blind forces of "civilization" that force him to dress, sing hymns, and eat distasteful food. In his own country, he felt a similar sympathy for the Negro throughout his mature life, and we find that in Huck's secret kinship with Jim, there is an instinctively shared savagery or resistance to civilization. In fact, Clemens' later sympathies for colored races were so strong that Mrs. Clemens gave her husband a convenient rule of thumb for saving his temper—to consider all men black until proved otherwise! Curiously enough, this feeling did not extend to the American Indian, aside from the Thanksgiving definition quoted in Chapter II. In *Roughing It* and *Life on the Mississippi*, he shows a fairly consistent animosity against them, which becomes full-blown in his attack on James Fenimore Cooper's idealization of the Red Man.

Volume II is far more colorful and lively, with all the brilliant hues and exotic lore of Ceylon and India. Although Twain is monumentally disappointed at the Taj Mahal—and vents an acid exasperation on guide books and travelers who build up one's expectations falsely—he responds to India with much of the old verve and dash that distinguish *The Innocents Abroad*.

By this time, his admiration for dark skin is extravagant:

> Nearly all black and brown skins are beautiful, but a beautiful white skin is rare. . . . Where dark complexions are massed, they make the whites look bleached out, unwholesome, and sometimes frankly ghastly. I could notice this as a boy, down South in the slavery days before the war. . . . Some of these [white] faces are pimply; some exhibit other signs of diseased blood; some show scars of a tint out of harmony with the surrounding shades of color. The white man's complexion makes no concealments. It can't. It seems to have been designed as a catch-all for everything that can damage it. Ladies have to paint it, and powder it, and cosmetic it, and diet it with arsenic, and enamel it, and be always enticing it, and persuading it, and pestering it, and fussing at it, to make it beautiful; and they do not succeed.

A wedding ceremony, Nautch dancers, a ride on an elephant, visits with holy men and royalty—he treats the reader to all the rich and gaudy spectacles. At Benares he surveys religious shrines and customs—including cremation—with the same Missouri skepticism that he exercised in Europe. Before he has finished, he has convinced the reader that "nothing has been left undone, either by man or Nature, to make India the most extraordinary country that the sun visits on his round."

Clemens was in his early sixties when this book appeared, and, for all its liveliness, it bears the marks of the pessimism of his later years. For one thing, there are continuing indications of his preoccupation with violence, suffering, and death, but without the comic overtones of such stories as "The Invalid's Tale." In *A Tramp Abroad* he spun out accounts of Alpine disasters, particularly the case in which a glacier rendered up the remains of several guides forty years after they fell into a fissure. In *Following the Equator* he is obsessed by the Australian savages who cauterize their own wounds or amputate their own wounded members. In India he lingers over the Towers of Silence, where the Parsee dead are exposed to the merciless efficiency of vultures and sunlight; the Suttee; the operations of Thugee murders; the bloodshed and agony at the Black Hole of Calcutta and the seiges of Cawnpore and Lucknow; and world statistics on death rates.

In addition, "Nature" becomes endowed with specifically malignant traits. In New Zealand, he saw a lignified caterpillar which, in entering its pupal stage, had been invaded by the spores of a peculiar fungus. "It happened not by accident, but by design—Nature's design. This caterpillar was in the act of loyally carrying out a law inflicted upon him by Nature—a law purposely inflicted upon him to get him into trouble—a law which was a trap. . . ." On the suggestion that the caterpillar suffered no pain, Clemens answers "If this one couldn't suffer, Nature would have known it and would have hunted up another caterpillar. Not that she would have let this one go, merely because it was defective. No. She would have waited and let him turn into a night-moth; and then fried him in the candle." A later observation confirms this devilish conspiracy:

It is strange and fine—Nature's lavish generosities to her creatures. At least to all of them except man. For those that fly she has provided a home that is nobly spacious—a home which is forty miles deep and envelops the whole globe, and has not an obstruction in it. For those that swim she has provided a more than imperial domain—a domain which is miles deep and covers four-fifths of the globe. But as for man, she has cut him off with the mere odds and ends of the creation. She has given him the thin skin, the meager skin which is stretched over the remaining one-fifth—the naked bones stick up through it in most places. On the one-half of this domain he can raise snow, ice, sand, rocks, and nothing else. So the valuable part of his inheritance really consists of but a single fifth of the family estate; and out of it he has to grub hard to get enough to keep him alive and provide kings and soldiers and powder to extend the blessings of civilization with. Yet man, in his simplicity and complacency and inability to cipher, thinks Nature regards him as the important member of the family—in fact, her favorite. Surely, it must occur to even his dull head, sometimes, that she has a curious way of showing it.

He closes this volume with a discussion of the Boer War and Jameson's raid on Johannesburg along with a visit to South African diamond mines.

❦

From the first New York impressions of a lively Western journalist to the embittered musings of an old man in India, Clemens' travel books survey art, customs, religions, sanitary conditions, history, dress, manners, methods of warfare, economics, transportation, legends, royalty, and scenery. The cultural assumptions from which he views this rich spectacle are predominantly those of an exceptionally humane nineteenth-century Protestant American businessman whose education is skimpy and whose theology has gone sour. His world-wide reputation and status as an author and reporter gave him entrance to many otherwise inaccessible shows, and especially during lecture tours, committees squired him around to see the sights. He usually had the money to travel in style, although that in itself may be a mixed blessing. His inveterate gregariousness brings onto the pages of the books hosts of varied people. In these books he remained true to the vow he made in his letter to Andrew Lang:

> I have never tried in even one single instance, to help cultivate the cultivated classes. I was not equipped for it, either by native gifts or training. And I never had any ambition in that direction, but always hunted for bigger game—the masses.

And in keeping his eye on this objective, he has reflected the ordinary assumptions of a class of Americans who did not find a voice in Henry James or Henry Adams.

5

≈§ HISTORICAL NOVELS

I N SETTING type for the Keokuk City Directory at his brother's printing firm—before he undertook any of the travels recorded in the preceding chapter—Samuel Clemens listed himself in bold-face type as "ANTIQUARIAN." We can see now that the joke had its prophetic aspect, since his historical writings are largely concerned with medieval and renaissance life. Throughout his travel writings, he shows a consciousness of history and its significance for contemporary life; and his historical novels are all set in foreign countries. Thus did his varied interests support each other. Some of his favorite works were Suetonius, Malory, St. Simon, and Carlyle and Dickens on the French Revolution.[1] Obviously the emphasis is on informal recollections and memoirs, the literary side of history, à la Pepys. Along with this interest goes a never diminishing absorption in costume and pageantry, mirrored by his own eccentricity of dress. His was delighted by colorful scenes in India and just as much by a gaudy parade such as he saw on Victoria's Jubilee. This interest reached its zenith in his enthusiasm over the historical pageant at Oxford when he went there to receive his honorary degree.

English history in particular, which is the subject of two of his historical novels, interested him greatly, so much so that in the

[1] Clemens read the *Memoirs* of Louis de Rouvroy, Duc de St. Simon (1675–1755), chronicler of court intrigue under Louis XIV and the regency of the Duc d'Orleans. It is not certain that he read Claude-Henri de Rouvroy, Comte de St. Simon (1760–1825), the first great leader of French socialism.

summer of 1883, during a period of idleness, he invented a game based on English history. It involved staking out proportionally exact spaces of land to represent the reign of each British monarch. His daughters were to gain fresh air and exercise while they unconsciously absorbed a perfectly proportioned sense of chronology.

We saw in Chapter I that his interest in astronomy and geology was strongly associated with a concern for relative *scales*. His interest, on the other hand, in the Swiftian exercise of reducing the immense or magnifying the tiny is based on a fascination with the absolute scale of time or of proportion by which the universe operates. And he always contemplated this scale with awe and wonderment. Again and again in the travel writings, this awe is invoked by the scale of time as he views the unrolling of history.

His interest in language is inseparable from his interest in scale, pageantry, and costume. Quaintness of style was one of Malory's primary appeals, and Clemens' own attempt to recreate archaic diction engaged both his sense of beauty and his sense of humor. These interests co-operated to concentrate his attention in history, with emphasis on the colorful medieval period, which gave scope as well for his idealism and his anti-romanticism.

We know the specific occasion for each of these books. The figure of Joan fascinated him from boyhood days. The journey of the Connecticut Yankee into King Arthur's England was immediately inspired by G. W. Cable's recommending a volume of Malory at a book store during the lecture tour of 1884–5, and the imbroglio experienced by the prince and the pauper grew at least in part out of a casual reading of Charlotte M. Yonge's *The Prince and the Page*. These subjects were doubtless made more attractive by Clemens' consciously calculated public restraint: he loved to rant and rage over injustice and cruelty, but he rarely permitted himself to publish such philippics on contemporary topics. He admits that he slipped now and then—particularly in public controversies over missionaries and over Christian Science— but he very carefully put most of his rantings into the *Autobiography* which was not to be made public until a hundred years after his death. In fuming over injustices of the distant past, however, he could indulge his temper gloriously without stepping on many toes.

This also gave him latitude for his anti-romanticism. We noted in Chapter III that Clemens blamed Sir Walter Scott's ersatz medievalism for the perverse and degenerate romanticism that he says caused the Civil War by deluding Southerners about the harsh contours of reality. Here was a perfect butt for ribbing and parodying the romantic exaggerations of what the period was like.

This sense of the discrepancy between appearance and reality we have named as the basis for Clemens' humor; it is also the deepest source of his humanitarian and moral stances. In the definition of Thanksgiving, he appears to be outraged at the smug, pious pre-conceptions with which the holiday is ordinarily greeted, and he uses the irony of satire to dispel the illusion that a very simple piety is all that motivated the original establishment of the holiday. *The Prince and the Pauper* and *Joan of Arc* are extended exercises in precisely the same pattern; one of the major aims of both books is the demonstration of the hypocrisy, greed, insensitivity, and barbarism that had become institutionalized in the laws, customs, churches and governments of sixteenth-century England and fifteenth-century France. In *A Connecticut Yankee*, he makes the same judgment on Arthurian England, but with the difference that a nineteenth-century mechanic is the agent who, through a miracle, goes back to that distant day to expose the discrepancies. Despite all the elaborate care and scholarship that went into the recreation of historical atmosphere, there lurks beneath the surface of all three books the assumption that late nineteenth-century American democracy has remedied most of those ills and that it is the ideal norm against which to measure the failure of other civilizations.

❦

Clemens began *The Prince and the Pauper* in the summer of 1877, after reading *The Prince and the Page*. As the idea originally presented itself to him, the period was to be modern, dealing with the childhood of Edward VII. We have seen that he did not wish to handle modern English life, having abandoned the proposed travel book on England in 1874. Indeed, we shall see in the following chapter that his treatment of contemporary life in novels was restricted to the American scene.

The desire to write a drama (which haunted Clemens as relentlessly as it did his very different contemporary, Henry James) re-asserted itself—it began in 1867 with an unfinished attempt to render *The Quaker City Holy Land Excursion* in play form. Perhaps because his comedy "Ah Sin," written in collaboration with Bret Harte a year earlier, and produced in May, 1877, had been such a severely qualified success, he determined to make *this* new play a richly gaudy costume piece, and to depend on that additional appeal for its commercial success. But the narrative form asserted itself, and he produced 400 manuscript pages before the summer was out. The book was then shelved for over two years; but on re-reading the manuscript later, he found its appeal continued, and he finished it, publishing the volume in 1882.

Work proceeded especially well during the summer of 1880, when the enthusiastic interest of his daughters and Olivia inspired him to work and probably shaped the character of the book. Also, he had been grinding away at the onerous task of padding out *A Tramp Abroad*, and this novel must have provided welcome relief and release. In his description of this work to Howells, he adds:

> Imagine *this* fact—I have even fascinated Mrs. Clemens with this yarn for youth. My stuff generally gets considerable damning with faint praise out of her, but this time it is all the other way. She is become the horse-leech's daughter, and my mill doesn't grind fast enough to suit her. That is no mean triumph, my dear sir.[2]

Even though he and Howells kept up an elaborate joke about the respective domination of their spouses, nevertheless, the firmness of Olivia's interest in this book cannot be doubted. Later she was to forbid its being published in one volume with the grubby Hannibal tale about Huck Finn, and insisted that *this* volume be lavishly decorated. It was she, too, who arranged, during Clemens' absence on his lecture tour with G. W. Cable, the Christmas performance of a family theatrical based on the novel, with roles performed by the Clemens daughters and children of their Hartford neighbors. The family passion for this tale continued, with Clemens later playing the role of Miles Hendon to Susy Clemens' prince.

Above all else it is a children's tale. The simplicity of mind that pervades the story is ideally suited to the blunt moral perceptions of children. One is reminded of the landlady in a short story of James Joyce, who is said to attack moral problems with a meat cleaver. The same is true of Clemens, notably in his own life when he discovered that during the family's absence, one of the servant girls had been cultivating the attentions of a tramp. When Clemens had the facts straight, he arranged a trap for the kitchen Don Juan, with the Rev. Joseph H. Twichell secreted in the bathroom, ready to pop out and marry the couple at the springing of the trap. Clemens' boyish glee in such amusements—and his iron-clad certainty of the moral uprightness of his position

---

[2] Albert Bigelow Paine, ed., *Mark Twain's Letters* (New York, Harper and Brothers, 1911), pp. 377–8.

—are the qualities that make *The Prince and the Pauper* what it is. Take, for example, this bit of characterization:

> 'My father, Sir Richard, is very rich, and of a most generous nature. My mother died whilst I was yet a boy. I have two brothers: Arthur, my elder, with a soul like to his father's; and Hugh, younger than I, a mean spirit, covetous, treacherous, vicious, underhanded—a reptile. . . . There is none other of us but the Lady Edith, my cousin—she was sixteen, then—beautiful, gentle, good, the daughter of an earl, the last of her race, heiress of a great fortune and a lapsed title.'

It has the ingenuousness of calendar art.

Tom Canty, son of a thief and grandson of a beggar, wanders from the squalor of Offal Court to Westminster, where he accidentally draws the attention of the nearly identical Edward, Prince of Wales. The prince calls him in and playfully exchanges clothing with the urchin. Accidentally the boys are separated, each out of his sphere; hereafter the tale alternates between the royal court and the filth of the underworld. This is perhaps Clemens' best organized book, because the multiple ironies in the situation are well marshaled. Each boy is arraigned by his supposed father and thought to be mad; each is befriended by the two sisters of his "twin"; each awakes from sleep thinking the mistake has been a dream, and so on.

In the meantime, Henry VIII dies and Tom is declared king. Edward, after being momentarily befriended by Miles Hendon, the previously exiled son of a noble, is taken up by a wandering gang of beggars and thieves who unwittingly give him a firsthand view of vice and poverty, and the economic conditions and laws that foster this development. At the same time, Tom saves a man, woman, and child from execution, repealing the law that calls for boiling alive as a penalty for murder by poisoning. The rightful king is tricked away from Miles by John Canty who assumes that this is his son and that he has a right to terrorize, bully, and profit from the boy. On escaping John's band of ruffians, Edward rests a day with a peasant woman before his encounter with a mad hermit who attempts to murder him in revenge for Henry VIII's dissolution of the monasteries.

In this particular scene, in which Miles comes breathlessly close to rescuing Edward, who nevertheless falls back into the outlaws' hands, Clemens attempts the classic melodramatic situation, evoking fear, anguish, and suspense. But the scene could hardly be anything but riotously ridiculous to a modern reader.

The reason for this is that he managed only moderately well with a form popular in his day; since then the particular clichés of melodrama that he so carefully imitated have become laughable. When the chuckling hermit, who grinds away at the rusty knife over the form of the bound but struggling and tearful boy, is compared to a loathsome spider, only the very young will shudder. After nearly being sentenced to death for stealing a pig (another instructive example of the harshness of his own laws) the mistaken king is reunited with Miles Hendon. They return to the latter's father's estate, only to be disowned by his cruel brother who has married Miles's fiancée during his exile. While Miles and Edward are in prison, Edward sees two Baptist women burned at the stake. Finally the pair escape to London, just in time to stop the coronation of Tom at its very climax. With Edward restored to his rights, the elaborately poetic justice of melodrama is worked out.

The plot of this novel had deep personal meaning for Clemens. A distant Lampton relative on his mother's side of the family wrote Clemens with some regularity, trying to enlist his help in establishing the Lampton right to the Earldom of Durham. This amused Clemens, and during his stay in London in 1873, he was fascinated by the classic lawsuit of the "Tichbourne claimant," requesting his secretary to keep voluminous scrapbooks of clippings on the trial. Psychologically, this concern with mistaken identity and claimants to noble rights can be seen as part of the general preoccupation with identity that we noted in Chapter II. It already found expression in the pseudonymous personality of the humorist and his friends, and will continue into many another book like *The American Claimant*.

Even more importantly, this novel is the first of an elaborate series of demonstrations, on Clemens' part, of the pervasive effect of environmental determinism over the rival claims of heredity. As several critics observe, the switching of roles shows that the prince becomes a humanitarian through directly experiencing the suffering of the common people, whereas the pauper becomes inured to the luxuries and idleness of the court to the extent that he ignores his own mother during one of his public appearances. Blair also observes that Clemens is in a sense carrying out a long-term debate with W. E. H. Lecky whose *History of European Morals* was one of his favorite books; it is Clemens' contention in *What Is Man?* that all moral action is selfishly motivated, and while Lecky recognizes this theory, he inclines toward the belief that an innate intuition is the basis of good action. In Edward's

73

Mark Twain

development of a moral sense through suffering and in Tom's comparative loss of a moral sense through luxury, Clemens is, in effect, showing Lecky to what extent one's personal status affects his moral judgments. Although his preoccupations shift with various books, Clemens continued a rich embroidery on this theme in *A Connecticut Yankee* where we shall see a factory mechanic becoming head of a nation and King Arthur becoming a slave; in the latter part of *Huckleberry Finn* where Huck and Tom exchange roles; in *The American Claimant* where a nobleman becomes a worker; and in *Pudd'nhead Wilson* where a slave becomes a master and a master a slave. This obsession continued into the unpublished manuscripts, where the theme of sexual reversal recurs, once with a pair composed of an effeminate boy and a tomboy girl.[3]

≈§ ई≈

The most immediately apparent difference between *The Prince and the Pauper* and *A Connecticut Yankee in King Arthur's Court* of 1889 is in the style. The Yankee's sojourn in sixth-century Britain is related here in a cracklingly profane and richly folksy first-person idiom that is perfectly suited to the Mencken-like diatribe against the age of chivalry. By Clemens' own suggestion, the Yankee foreman from the Hartford Colt Factory is a Robinson Crusoe—set down in a brutal, childlike society rotten with the effects of superstition, ignorance, and absolute government. He quietly sets up newspapers, schools, fire departments, insurance companies, a mint, a patent system, a West Point and a naval academy, telephone and telegraph communication, Protestant churches, and traveling soap missionaries to convert people to bathing. Clemens' Yankee, Hank Morgan, represents the inherent assumptions of late nineteenth-century American businessman's democracy as well as Defoe's eighteenth-century castaway represents the British bourgeois values of that day. And from the beginning, it is the manner of the account which most subtly and effectively conditions the reader.

If the story of Edward VI is melodrama, *A Connecticut Yankee* is, refreshingly enough, a "novel of ideas," and should be considered alongside the efforts of Aldous Huxley in the same genre, or G. B. Shaw in drama. It has even closer affinities with Upton

3 Kenneth S. Lynn, *Mark Twain and Southwestern Humor* (Boston, Little, Brown and Co., 1959), pp. 260–1, 272.

Sinclair or Bellamy (who sends his observer into a future utopia rather than an obsolete past).

The book follows no particular party line (aside from the suggestion that some aspects are meant as a defense of Grover Cleveland's administration); it is rather Clemens' own unique refraction of many of the values of his age and environment. With his superior knowledge and mechanical skill, the ingenious Hank Morgan immediately builds a reputation as a magician that gives him the title of "The Boss." He reforms a whole nation according to the tastes of the sage of Hannibal and Hartford. Personal comfort is as important to him as literacy or anti-Catholicism; the predominant drift of ideas is toward a benevolent, gadget-infested, bustling active industrial democracy. The closest he approaches to doctrinaire didacticism is in The Boss's impassioned defense of Free Trade to a group of benighted Protectionists in Chapter XXXIII.

Clemens was acquainted with Cervantes, and certainly minor incidents here and there, such as the bewitched drove of pigs, recall *Don Quixote*. But the basic situation is the opposite of that in the Spanish classic, since here the hero is the only sane person in a nation of fools, children, and schemers. It is Malory's *Morte d'Arthur* which really sired this satire. Clemens loved the volume, and read it repeatedly, but at least as much for amusement as for enchantment. Long passages in *A Connecticut Yankee* are devoted to burlesquing the style and ideas of this manual of chivalry. Fred W. Lorch has pointed out the additional possibility that an earlier uncompleted novel on feudalism in Hawaii may have given Clemens some of the ideas used in this novel.

Religion is treated largely in Chapters XXI–XXIII, during the Boss's visit to the Valley of Holiness. In general, Clemens tends to view the Catholic Church as an absolutistic, despotic organization that fosters ignorance and superstition and that participates at the side of the nobles in pillaging the helpless masses. W. E. H. Lecky certainly parallels him in some of these attitudes.

Indeed, Clemens informs us that many of the details of Morgan's sojourn in the Valley of Holiness are drawn from Lecky's denunciation of asceticism. The performance centers on the early desert monks to the exclusion of any other evidence. Lecky describes the bowing in prayer of St. Stylite on his pillar; the practical Hank Morgan attaches a power take-off to the saint, and uses his movement as power to run sewing machines to produce shirts. Clemens' clownish prejudice is indicated by his preoccupation with hoary jokes like the Bishop's desiring the *droit du seigneur*, or the monastery on one hill, the convent on the other, and a foundling hospital between the two. In this particular narration, a fountain in the Valley has failed soon after the monks bathed, leading them to suppose that baths are sinful. After Merlin the magician ignominiously fails to restore the spring, the Yankee succeeds spectacularly by plugging up a leak in the well, to the accompaniment of an impressive display of Greek fire, rockets, and roman candles.

The political doctrines of The Boss consist of a wholehearted defense of democracy on the standard American pattern of his day—universal male suffrage and separation of church and state. At the lowest level, it is simply a matter of sermonizing and bald statement: "any Established Church is an established crime, an established slave-pen," or "where every man in a State has a vote, brutal laws are impossible." He excoriates royalty, nobility, and aristocracy in harangues that make up in vituperation for what they lack in support, reasoning, or objectivity. In liberating what King Arthur's culture facetiously calls "freemen," The Boss specifically abjures revolution on the pattern of Jack Cade or Wat Tyler on the grounds of inefficiency—education is the prerequisite to revolution, he says. His answer is to set up a "Man Factory" for the production of Lecky's kind of Protestant.

Midway in the volume, in Chapters XXVII to XXXVIII, Clemens resorts to the "schizophrenic" change of identity device he employed in *The Prince and the Pauper* when King Arthur voluntarily disguises himself as a yeoman and travels incognito among his subjects. Clemens runs through his familiar comic tricks on problems of identity. The Boss has no end of difficulty at first in training the king to stoop his shoulders, look to the ground, and show the manifold traits of oppression. Although The Boss is properly horrified by the injustice, cruelty, and backwardness they encounter, it is not until they are both sold as slaves that King Arthur vows to abolish at least that social crime from his realm. Clemens descends periodically to the kind of meretriciously bathetic sentimentality that mars the story of Tom and Edward. Particularly in such scenes as the burning of a woman at the stake during a snow storm in order to keep a band of slaves from perishing of cold, and the hanging of a nursing mother for petty theft, Clemens might have hit the apogee of late nineteenth-century popular art, but it is embarrassing to read today. Luckily such scenes do not dominate the volume, although in his treatment of the in-

Brown Brothers

Clemens' House in Hartford

77

credible cruelties of Morgan le Fay, one almost suspects Clemens of parodying himself.

The same problem arises where melodrama is concerned. Certainly it dominates the imbroglio in London whereby, after a misfired revolt, the slaves are to be hanged. They are saved only at the last minute, when the noose is already around Arthur's neck, by Lancelot and a troop of knights who arrive on bicycle. Plausibility is stretched so far, and Clemens' execution is so slipshod, that one is tempted to see this whole episode, too, as a satiric attack on melodrama. But the explanation is too subtle. As we shall see in the parody attacks on sentimentality in the Grangerford episodes of *Huckleberry Finn,* Clemens is incapable of such fine discriminations. His idea of a comic method is like the well-known advice of the Irishman on the use of the shillelagh, "When you see a head, hit it." In a sense, the melodrama here is too preposterously managed even to be taken as satire. Besides, in the aesthetic economy of his day, sentimentality is an inherent part of the melodrama, and it is impossible that he meant us to take the sentimental portions of the story seriously and the melodramatic portions lightly.

The climax on the scaffold in Chapter XXXVIII is capped by The Boss's defeating the flower of English chivalry in a joust by using his cowboy lasso and revolvers. Then the book takes another turn in the last five chapters. Morgan is tricked into a long voyage, supposedly for his daughter's health, during which England is torn by internecine feudal warfare, followed by an Interdict imposed by the Church. A pitched battle ensues between The Boss, his trusty aide Clarence, and fifty-four hand-picked boys against the rest of the nation. Blowing up all his factories, schools, and remaining civilized improvements in self-defense, Hank Morgan, isolated on an artificially created island, grimly dynamites and electrocutes 25,000 knights, whereupon all his camp die of the resultant poisoned air. The brutal extravagance of the night scenes in which troop after troop of knights are silently impaled on the electric fences, comes as a distinct surprise. However wide the range of aesthetic effects earlier in the book, there was nothing to prepare the reader for this grim horror. Even though Clemens was deeply concerned, perhaps by now disgusted, with the continuing expenses of the Paige typesetter the dynamite ending does not suggest a repudiation of an industrial economy; it is the first of Clemens' major blasts at the "damned human race." The invincible stupidity and viciousness of the medieval English, even in the face of Hank Morgan's wholesale reforms, necessitates the complete destruction of his new civilization. The people are not worthy of the system.

In the postscript, Twain himself in the nineteenth century witnesses the pathetic death of Morgan who now wishes he were back in the sixth century with his wife and child. Like many another of his books, this is a fantastic hodgepodge; one agrees easily with A. B. Paine that "As an example of Mark Twain at his literary worst and best the *Yankee* ranks supreme."

Although illustrations in the first editions of all of Clemens' works are interesting and usually of high quality, Dan Beard's work for this volume surpasses most of the other efforts. The pictures reproduce the tone of violent burlesque and buffoonery, frequently with allegorical overtones. In a copy in the J. K. Lilly collection at the Indiana University Library, Beard has identified his models in the margins. The Boss is drawn from a young photoengraver who worked next door to Beard's studio; Clarence is patterned after Sarah Bernhardt; Merlin is Alfred Lord Tennyson; King Arthur is the Kaiser; and the slave driver is Jay Gould!

A Connecticut Yankee was composed over a period of several years, beset by many interruptions and distractions. Clemens wrote portions of it at the home of his friend Twichell, to the accompaniment of loud noises from children at play and carpenters remodeling the house. As noted above, it was written during a period of severe financial strain, when the Paige typesetter was devouring money ravenously; at times, Clemens vowed to race through the book so that he would finish it at the same time the typesetter was completed. But perhaps the most salient influence on the composition was Clemens' burning rages against Matthew Arnold for criticizing General Grant's grammar and America.[4]

In addition, there were difficulties with the British publisher, who was chary about printing the work, and with the critics, who attacked it viciously in some instances. Clemens was hurt and annoyed at this response, and wrote to Andrew Lang to request that this friend do something to right his reputation. His letter, quoted in Chapter I, is a classically simple apologia that is perhaps the best possible defense of his work as a whole. Lang, however, could not bring himself to praise the *Yankee*, and in his article on Clemens lavished praise where it belongs, on *Huckleberry Finn*.

[4] One is reminded here of Matthew Arnold's classic remark to Mrs. Howells when he heard that her husband was collaborating with Mark Twain on a comic play: "Oh, but he doesn't like *that* sort of thing, does he?" Paine, *Biography*, p. 758.

❧ ☙

Clemens' early interest in Joan during his days in Hannibal grew out of an accident in which the wind blew into his hands a page from a book describing Joan's torture by the English. Even before he knew anything about French history, he was inflamed with an intense sympathy for this mistreated girl.

He was quite right in considering his *Joan of Arc* a companion volume to *The Prince and the Pauper* since the books share that peculiarly sweetened and reverent idealism that so delighted the Clemens women and the dominant taste of the day. While the exigencies of literal history hampered him in fabricating those heightened melodramatic climaxes that mar the other two history books, the figure of Joan gave him complete license to indulge his worship of virgin purity that we saw him exalting in his various clubs for young girls. And when Joan in Chapter XII requires the boisterous and foul-mouthed Captain LaHire to rid the camp of prostitution and drinking, to make his men attend two masses daily, and to amend his own profane speech, she is doing precisely what the Clemens women performed in what they called "dusting off Papa."

Clemens knew that this book was out of his ordinary line. It was serialized in *Harper's* as an anonymous production, since he feared that his *nom de plume* on *The Prince and the Pauper* obscured the true qualities of the volume and led readers to look for kinds of humor and irreverence which he did not intend.

The book contains other interesting anomalies. In worshipping at this shrine Clemens was forced to make at least temporary peace with the French nation and the Catholic Church, two of the greatest *bêtes noires* of his whole career, although he does permit himself to lavish hatred on "that bastard of Satan, Pierre Cauchon, Bishop of Beauvais" and other particular churchmen. In the trial he had to make out his beloved English to be the villains. Thus the volume can be said to hold in suspension some very deep tensions. It is Clemens' bland refusal to face or investigate these tensions that makes this book such a perplexing document.

Joan obviously represents, as a figure, the symbolic identification of national and religious feelings of her age, which was later to issue in the theory of the divine right of kings. Clemens was aware of the difficulties this subject presented to one of his beliefs, and he takes particular glee in excoriating both the nobility and the priests for their treatment of Joan, overlooking the fact that all her sacrifices and martyrdom were in the service of and for the greater glory of the king and the religion. Although he exalts her at the end as an allegory for patriotism, he nowhere indicates the total value of the nation or the ideals for which the patriotism is expended, except for the sentimental memories of a small-town childhood. As George Bernard Shaw very ably points out in the preface to his "Saint Joan," one must inherently understand "Christendom and the Catholic Church, the Holy Roman Empire and the Feudal System, as they existed and were understood in the Middle Ages" in order to approach such a subject.

> If you confuse the Middle Ages with the Dark Ages . . . and are quite convinced that the world has progressed enormously, both morally and mechanically, since Joan's time, then you will never understand why Joan was burnt, much less feel that you might have voted for burning her yourself if you had been a member of the court that tried her; and until you feel that you know nothing essential about her.
>   That the Mississippi pilot should have broken down on this misunderstanding is natural enough. Mark Twain, the Innocent Abroad, who saw the lovely churches of the Middle Ages without a throb of emotion, author of A Yankee at the Court of King Arthur, in which the heroes and heroines of medieval chivalry are guys seen through the eyes of a street arab, was clearly out of court from the beginning.[5]

What Clemens tries to present, then, is a tacitly detached character study which worships tremblingly and reverently the moral stature of the woman without any reference to the specific ends she expended all her efforts to effect. This is not to say that Clemens ignores Joan's voices or her dedication to a worthless king; he simply presents them as brute surface facts without any depth of analysis or belief behind them. This results in moralizing in a vacuum.

The simplicity of this approach brings to the fore other qualities of Clemens' thought which are obvious in the travel literature and elsewhere. When he is convinced of the truth of a proposition, he pursues it with the inflexibility and earnestness of the indomitable salesman. This is seen in his habitual use of superlatives like these:

> She was perhaps the only entirely unselfish person whose name has a place in profane history.

[5] *Plays,* Ayot St. Lawrence Edition (New York, Wm. H. Wise and Co., 1930, Vol. XVII), p. 27.

The details of the life of Joan of Arc form a biography which is unique among the world's biographies in one respect: *It is the only story of a human life which comes to us under oath,* the only one which comes to us from the witness stand.

It took six thousand years to produce her; her like will not be seen in the earth again in fifty thousand.

. . . the most noble life that was ever born into this world save only One.

The American business pusher stands, too, behind numerous passages in which the style is a blend of superficial and falsely poetic cliché metaphors and gusty businessman's lingo. For example, the following representative sentence moves directly from the fake poetry to the Babbitt jargon: "And nobody could help cheering, she was such a vision of young bloom and beauty and grace, and such an incarnation of pluck and life and go!" [6]

For the most part, he attempts to gain a grand manner by excessive parallelism and repetition, both in dialogue and in narration:

'You shall live—and you shall serve France—'
'I will serve *you!*'
—'you shall fight for France—'
'I will fight for *you!*'
'You shall be France's soldier—'
'I will be *your* soldier!'
—'you shall give all your heart to France—'
'I will give all my heart to *you*—and all my soul, if I have one—and all my strength, which is great—for I was dead and am alive again; I had nothing to live for, but now I have! You are France for me. You are my France, and I will have no other.'

The organization is reminiscent of the double plot of *The Prince and the Pauper.* Clemens alternates, in the first half of the book, between the achievements of Joan in war and the mock heroics of

---

[6] Contrast the falseness of diction in this passage with the following from *Connecticut Yankee,* in which nineteenth-century Americanisms and the extended mining metaphor have a functional meaning within the satiric context. Morgan is disgusted at the Demoiselle Alisande La Careloise for a fantastic tale she has delivered to the King: "Oh, well, it was reasonably plain, now, why these donkeys didn't prospect these liars for details. It may be that this girl had a fact in her somewhere, but I don't believe you could have sluiced it out with a hydraulic; nor got it with the earlier forms of blasting, even, it was a case for dynamite. Why, she was a perfect ass; and yet the king and his knights had listened to her as if she had been a leaf out of the gospel. It kind of sizes up the whole party. And think of the simple ways of this court: this wandering wench hadn't any more trouble to get access to the king in his palace than she would have had to get into the poorhouse in my day and country. In fact, he was glad to see her, glad to hear her tale; with that adventure of hers to offer, she was as welcome as a corpse is to a coroner."

a childhood friend, Paladin. Paladin is a braggart as old as the *miles gloriosus,* with strong affinities, of course, to the Shakespearian Falstaff. But obviously Clemens' immediate source was the mining and frontier community liar. Before long, he tempers his sharpness by making Paladin into a lovable entertainer whose exploits as Joan's standard-bearer now and then entail real bravery. It is intersting, in fact, to note that Joan is specifically dedicated to nullifying the provisions of the Treaty of Troyes, made by her English heroic counterpart Henry V. That she does not abjure her youthful companion Paladin, for all his lying, but converts him into a useful servant—unlike Henry V's treatment of Falstaff—is the index of Clemens' widely noted "tenderness" in his approach to this subject.

The second half of the book relies heavily on Quicherat's transcription of the trials and the rehabilitation proceedings which later redeemed her reputation. However, Clemens also indulges in copious moralizing.

Joan is praised for her peasant simplicity, practicality, and directness, for the vigorous and blunt way in which she confounded the greatest minds of her century, and for the inflexible and inspiring force of her convictions, allied with pure selflessness. These are the ideals that drew Clemens to her, and in presenting these qualities he is at his best.

In other respects, he wavers. Charles VII is usually referred to as an "ingrate" or a "treacherous dog," and yet in Chapter XXXVIII, when he sides with Joan against his own counsellors, he is presented sympathetically. Many times, in treating Paladin's bragging, Clemens is insensibly drawn into what would otherwise have been a vulgarly comic situation, but he wavers and then compromises, and ends on an equivocal tone that leaves the reader wondering. He obviously was curbing the natural tendency of his inspiration at these points. Even in the famous anecdote of Joan's uncle riding to the funeral on the bull that crashed into a beehive, the material is presented with a chastened and apologetic tone. Since this yarn was one of the staples of Southwestern humor, having served as a vehicle for Sut Lovingood, among others, its presence in this book may well represent the farthest reach of American folk humor into the realm of genteel Victorian belles-lettres.

But the greatest wavering is to be seen in the character of the narrator, the Sieur de Conte. Clemens obviously used this figure to absolve himself from having to take the Catholic faith and French patriotism seriously; and de Conte dutifully mouths the sentiments and notions that a man of his station and age could be expected to hold. However, every now and then he lapses into egregiously Twainian attitudes that are again lost equivocally between reverence, suppressed boisterousness, and deterministic pessimism. In the following pargraphs, for example, there is a haunting flavor of mining-camp camaraderie and violent frontier humor, and yet Clemens knows that it is inappropriate, and tones it down to a puzzlingly gentle meaninglessness:

> The boys were amazed that I could make such a poem as that out of my own head, and so was I, of course, it being as much a surprise to me as it could be to anybody, for I did not know that it was in me. . . .
>
> That is the way with us; we may go on half of our life not knowing such a thing is in us, when in reality it was there all the time, and all we needed was something to turn up that would call for it. Indeed, it was always so with our family. My grandfather had a cancer, and they never knew what was the matter with him till he died, and he didn't himself. It is wonderful how gifts and diseases can be concealed that way. All that was necessary in my case was for this lovely and inspiring girl to cross my path, and out came the poem, and no more trouble to me to word it and rhyme it and perfect it than it is to stone a dog. No, I should have said it was not in me; but it was.
>
> The boys couldn't say enough about it, they were so charmed and astonished.

And yet the girl in question, Catherine Boucher, is presented in Clemens' most sentimental manner.

⤢ ⤣

Clemens indulged in what has been called "polymorphic composition." He simply let his pen fly almost at its own will, and moved effortlessly from sentiment to corrosive satire, and from parody to commercial statistics. This same spirit of total freedom of movement shines forth in *Connecticut Yankee,* which represents all that is authentic and enduring in Clemens' historical fiction because it is the only volume in which his personality is given free rein. In the person of Hank Morgan, he is on home ground, defending the preassumptions of his background and environment, and glorying in his satiric attacks and burlesque on all that he finds evil and meretricious in medieval society and art.

The Prince and the Pauper and *Joan of Arc* may be unfortunate victims of a change in taste; their sentimentality and melodrama are repellent to the modern palate, although they were probably real enough achievements in their day. The shallowness of moral judgments and the simplicity with which reality is represented are, however, inalienable components of that contemporary vogue in art, and it is for these qualities that one finds it hard to forgive Clemens.

In short, the true Mark Twain sparkles on the pages of his Arthurian hoax; the style has that gusty and earthly irreverence that we associate with his newspaper writings; the episodic, joking anecdote is the basis for the organization; and hardheaded materialism pervades the whole performance. The masterstroke, however, is the same one that makes *Huckleberry Finn* superior to *Tom Sawyer:* when he is really at his ease, Clemens works best with first-person narration. This is a demonstration of the profound relevance of certain stylistic devices to certain philosophic and psychological commitments—for the deepest significance of democratic individualism, only the first-person point of view gives full play to his Missouri skepticism and his inflexible pragmatism.

It was perhaps a sense of kinship with this same democratic pragmatism that Franklin D. Roosevelt recalled when he said he first found the phrase "New Deal" in the pages of this novel.

6

❧ AMERICAN NOVELS

THE IMMEDIATE appeal of *A Connecticut Yankee* in contrast to the other historical novels suggests that Clemens is at his best in dealing with home subjects and familiar surroundings, when he can speak out in his own voice, heedless of that segment of contemporary taste which insisted on genteel propriety. His treatment of relatively contemporary American material brings him closer to the Mark Twain who lives in the public heart. In *The Gilded Age* (1873) he and Charles Dudley Warner epitomized the whole fevered epoch of financial speculation following the Civil War. The character of Colonel Beriah Sellers was so popular in the stage adaptation of this novel that he attempted in *The American Claimant* (1892) to carry on Sellers' adventures, although he actually succeeded in writing a novel on the troubles of young lovers torn between democratic equalitarianism and a British title. Both of these novels, as we shall see, draw heavily on relatives and family reminiscences. *Pudd'nhead Wilson* and *Those Extraordinary Twins* (1894) carry Clemens back to Missouri and the kind of town he grew up in. In dealing with the fortunes of slaves and the pretensions of the immigrant Virginia aristocracy, he is moving back to the issues of his childhood. Finally, we can include in this discussion the bulk of the short stories, which deal largely with American subjects.

All these works are of uneven quality, containing much that is delightful and profound, mixed in with buffoonery and high melodrama. *Pudd'nhead Wilson* ranks close to *The Prince and the Pauper* as a concentrated, unified novel, with *The Gilded Age* a close second, although it has its irrelevancies and contradictions. *The American Claimant* is, in one way, a hilarious example of the violence that can result from a zealous use of the method of humorous discrepancies: it resembles some of the short stories in the way that it yokes together the most incredibly garish contrasting elements. On the whole, the short stories must rank very high in the Twain canon; one or two of them, which we shall consider in the last chapter, are among the greatest to come from his (or any American) pen. In length they are admirably suited to the anecdote and in content to a genially colloquial style. There is less room in them for meandering off into side issues, unless, as is sometimes the case, such meandering is the comic point of the tale. They are close to his personal experience, and they give us the most intimate and heart-warming picture of the true Mark Twain. It is curious that until Mr. Charles Neider's recent edition, no one had ever thought of collecting them into one volume. They make, in fact, one of the most thoroughly satisfying books to come from Twain's hand, with the usual exception of *Huckleberry Finn*.

The Gilded Age began almost as a parlor amusement. One evening in Hartford when the Charles Dudley Warners were dinner guests, the gentlemen attacked the current harvest of novels so vociferously that the ladies challenged them to turn out something superior themselves. Clemens and Warner, both successful writers and both unoccupied at the moment, accepted the gambit and set about planning a novel which would challenge the tyranny of feminine taste in that form. They worked from February to April, 1873. The result is a book bristling with current scandal, varied characters, big doings, and genuinely funny developments. Clemens' biographer, A. B. Paine, says that the two men divided the work fairly equally, each producing about half the chapters; most scholars, however, tend to give Clemens major credit for the conception. He had already planned the early part before the dinner conversation, and we shall see that it parallels Clemens' family history closely. The detailed material on Washington must be drawn from Clemens' days as secretary to Senator Stewart and as a syndicated columnist in the capital. All the humor bears his authoritative mark.

They got their friend J. Hammond Trumbull to provide very

scholarly-looking chapter mottoes taken from nearly every language and system of writing the world has ever known. They would have done better simply to preface the volume with this paragraph from Chapter XXVI:

> Beautiful credit! The foundation of modern society. Who shall say that this is not the golden age of mutual trust, of unlimited reliance upon human promises? That is a peculiar condition of society which enables a whole nation to instantly recognize point and meaning in the familiar newspaper anecdote, which puts into the mouth of a distinguished speculator in lands and mines this remark: 'I wasn't worth a cent two years ago, and now I owe two millions of dollars.'

The Gilded Age, as they see it, is a quagmire of labyrinthine financial speculations, flimsy credit, and paper value, gilded over by fancy oratory, fake advertisements, pious sentiments, and opium dreams of quick riches. And a Congress crying out to be bribed, bartered, and bought is the quicksand at the center of the swamp.

The early life of John Clemens, Sam's father, is reflected in Squire (later Judge) Hawkins' marriage in Kentucky and his settling in Tennessee, where he purchases the tract of land that led to such fabulous dreams. There follows the enthusiastic letter from Colonel Beriah Sellers that lures the family to Missouri. Sellers, the irrepressible dreamer who lives in an aura of imagined wealth and financial prospects as thickly impenetrable as the chivalric fog that envelops Don Quixote, is based in part on Clemens' uncle, John Quarles, who wrote a similar letter to get the Clemenses to Missouri. But the real basis of this celebrated portrait is James Lampton, a cousin on Sam's mother's side. The untimely death of Judge Hawkins, who murmurs about the future wealth to be gained from the Tennessee land even as he expires, is precisely the picture we have of John Clemens in the *Autobiography*.

Here the close resemblance to the family history slacks off, except for the splendid portrait of Orion Clemens, the ebullient, ineffective, and lovable dreamer, in the character of Washington Hawkins. Clemens used his own river experience in Chapters III and IV in the description of the steamboat race and the explosion of the *Aramanth*, patterned after the destruction of the *Pennsylvania* in which Sam's Brother Henry perished.

Two young Easterner surveyors, Philip Sterling and Henry Brierly, come to Missouri to cash in on the railroad boom, where they are taken in by Colonel Sellers' wild dream of developing

Stone's Landing into a metropolis called Napoleon by bringing in the railroad. He also means to deepen, straighten, and lengthen a little stream called Goose Run, then to be renamed the Columbus River. This scheme bears close resemblance to Judge Clemens' presidency of a short-lived company that was dedicated to making the Salt River navigable in order to revitalize the hamlet of Florida.

Following the same penchant for dealing in paired characters which we have already discussed in the historical novels, Philip turns out to be an ambitious, steady worker, whereas his friend Henry is the empty braggart, dupe and duper of all the unscrupulous speculators. Henry has an amorous interest in Laura Hawkins, an orphan of the *Aramanth* disaster who was adopted by the family on their way to Missouri. After being tricked into a false marriage by Colonel Selby, a Confederate officer who hardheartedly deserts her after three months, she becomes a calculating charmer who uses her beauty as Henry uses his tongue, to inflame and then capitalize on the gullibility of suckers.

In its early sections, the book is only loosely organized, and it often stops in mid-passage for delicious little set pieces like the exciting steamboat disaster, the Negro corpse in the dissecting room, and the richly humorous description of the muddy, venal, and corrupt city of Washington in Chapter XXIV. For all this seemingly irrelevant material, there is a thematic undercurrent which unites the most varied characters and situations in the fever for quick wealth. It is perplexing that Clemens should have portrayed the delusions of this state of mind so penetratingly in 1873 and then got caught up in the Paige Typesetter whirlpool from 1880–94. The only explanation is that to know one's own weaknesses is not an automatic cure; as his biographer says,

> He had no moral right to be connected with business at all. He had a large perception of business opportunity, but no vision of its requirements—its difficulties and details. He was the soul of honor, but in anything resembling practical direction he was but a child.[1]

Colonel Sellers mapping out the course of the railroad with assorted household objects on the dinner table, Laura calculating how to rise fast in Washington society through a judicious use of sexual lures, and the President of the Columbus River Slackwater Navigation Company explaining in his oily and cynical manner

[1] Albert Bigelow Paine, *Mark Twain, A Biography* (New York, Harper and Brothers, 1912), p. 728.

how to bribe an appropriations bill through Congress—these are fascinating psychological analyses of obsession.

The structure tightens up about midway when the story turns to the schemes of Laura and Senator Dilworthy. They want to pass an appropriation bill that will sell or lease the Hawkins Tennessee lands to the government for Knobs Industrial University, a Negro institution. Needless to say, the Hawkinses would be millionaires overnight. At the same time, Colonel Sellers pushes the Columbus River Improvement Program, while Philip Sterling attempts to dig coal out of John Bolton's Pennsylvania land.

When Laura re-encounters her former seducer, Colonel Selby, she resumes her intimacy with him. The Knobs Industrial University bill is passing in the House of Representatives after a bitterly contested battle, at the very time that Laura is in New York, pursuing Selby, who means to escape to Europe with wife and children. She confronts him at the Southern Hotel and shoots him dead.

A second major climax occurs as Laura is acquitted of the murder on the grounds of temporary insanity. Her ill-fated attempt at lecturing is followed by a fatal heart attack. The legal loophole of the insanity plea, which allowed the accused to go free without even a suggestion of psychotherapy, was a contemporary abuse that Clemens excoriated whenever he got a chance. He also takes the opportunity in this novel to condemn the excesses of the jury system of trial. Chronologically, this is the first of the great trial scenes with which Clemens loved to climax his novels—*Tom Sawyer; Pudd'nhead Wilson; Tom Sawyer, Detective;* and *The Mysterious Stranger*.

Back home at the meeting of the State Legislature, Dilworthy attempts to bribe Mr. Noble, the opposition leader, to secure his own nomination as Senator. Noble seems to accept the money, but then dramatically exposes the offer to the Legislature by throwing the $7,000 on the Speaker's table. But like Laura, Dilworthy is practically exonerated by the Senate for the short remainder of his term in office.

The conception of the whole novel, we remember, was a male protest against feminine taste in fiction. The subtitle, *A Tale of Today,* announces the authors' intention to deal in realism. There are, here and there, indications that Clemens and Warner were in conscious revolt against certain romantic conventions of the novels popular in their day. They lead the reader on false scents, but suddenly reverse the train of events to say what happened in reality, in contradistinction to what ordinarily happens in novels. In the joking appendix, they apologize for not having found Laura's still-missing father, explaining "We supposed, from the ease with which lost persons are found in novels, that it would not be difficult."

But what they primarily depended on for their masculine concept of reality was two notorious scandals that had received wide publicity. The facts of Laura's later career as murderess and lecturer were drawn from the case of Laura Fear, a celebrated San Francisco murderess. Since she had earlier lived in Virginia City, some feel there is a possibility Clemens might actually have met her. The nearly fantastic drama of Senator Dilworthy's exposure is a literal transcription of the career of Senator Samuel Clarke Pomeroy (1816–91) of Kansas which vied for attention with other open sores in the Reconstruction Congress. In addition, the Tweed Ring is rather obviously satirized in William Weed and his gang.

The Prince and the Pauper, Tom Sawyer, and *The American Claimant* all presented themselves to Clemens' imagination at one time or another as possible dramas; in the process of writing, the first two turned into novels and were published in that form, being dramatized only at a later time. The third work alone reached completion as a drama before Clemens wrote a novel on the subject. Perhaps the idea stemmed from the great financial success of *The Gilded Age* which was dramatized in 1874. At any rate, he and Howells collaborated on *Colonel Sellers as a Scientist* in 1883, guffawing and cutting up like schoolboys as they concocted the fantastic scenes. This was to be a kind of sequel to *The Gilded Age,* retaining Washington Hawkins and Colonel Sellers, who is now claimant to the Earldom of Rossmore.[2] We remember that a distant cousin on his mother's side fought a lifelong battle for recognition as the rightful Earl of Durham. The vogue of Spiritualism, which Clemens commented on as a San Francisco journalist, and which permeated the Nook Farm circle in Hartford, was used in Colonel Sellers' attempt to materialize spirits. Before the

---

[2] The original was named Eschol Sellers, but when an actual person of that name threatened a law suit, subsequent editions of *The Gilded Age* contained the name Beriah Sellers; when the play appeared, an actual Beriah forced the change to Mulberry Sellers, which has not been challenged!

play reached production, Howells despaired of it, and it never got beyond one-night stands in outlying towns.

In beginning the novel version, Clemens thought he could use large portions of the play, but because new ideas crowded out the incidents from the drama, he was disappointed; it is said, however, that Chapter III contains typical material from the play.

The American Claimant represents Clemens' riotous imagination pushed almost to the point of self-parody. Colonel Sellers' plan to materialize dead policemen to replace the present New York force at a great profit to himself is typical of the schemes that are a kind of hysterical expansion of the financial speculations of *The Gilded Age*. To balance Sellers' high-flown ambitions as the rightful claimant to a British title, Clemens brings the young heir to the usurped British title to America. Viscount Berkeley, fired up with democratic and equalitarian zeal, has determined to make his way in the world unaided. He escapes a hotel fire, in his haste putting on the clothes of One-Armed Pete, a Western desperado whom Sellers and Hawkins have been tracking for reward money. On each day that he fails to find employment, his republican zeal diminishes. Under the pseudonym of Howard Tracy, the young nobleman is obviously a vehicle for Clemens' increasingly virulent didactic strain; the author even uses the transparent device of sending Tracy to a mechanics' debate group, where he hears a paper by a journalist who trounces Matthew Arnold. Then a self-educated printer and clerk extols practical, workaday knowledge of the sort that inventors develop. The speech is full of violent statements such as the assertion that "this century, the only century worth living in since time itself was invented, is the creation of men not college-bred." Clemens' personal prejudices stand behind these opinions as modestly as would a mountain range.

But there is rewarding ore cached away here and there in the form of squibs and comic situations where the true Mark Twain geniality and bite shine forth. In Chapter IX, for example, he belabors the penchant of actresses to gain fame by pretending to have lost valuable diamonds in hotel fires. Then Sellers, who thinks Viscount Berkeley was killed in one of three places in the hotel, collects three baskets of ashes. This gives Clemens *carte blanche* to indulge in his beloved graveyard humor, in the debate about how to send the three baskets back to England, which basket contains the nobleman, and kindred complications.

The two strands are united when Tracy wanders into Sellers' yard wearing One-Armed Pete's clothes. Sellers has meanwhile been trying to materialize the spirit of the desperado, and when he sees that Tracy has two arms, an English accent, and gentle manners, he assumes that through a hitch in the process, he has materialized one of Pete's ancestors. On repeated visits, Tracy and Sellers' daughter Sally fall deeply in love. Tracy writes to his father confessing he has had his fill of working-class self-sufficiency; he proposes to resume his aristocratic position and to marry Sally, thus restoring the Earldom to its rightful heirs. As the Earl embarks for America, Sellers and his wife prepare to sail for England, newly rich on the profits of a "pig in the clover" puzzle that Sellers invented.

After a series of involved melodramatics, in which Hawkins develops fantastic plans to prevent Sally's marriage to what he assumes is a materialized spirit, the youngsters marry while Sellers is off on a new scheme to change weather throughout the world and to establish a republic in Siberia with the proceeds.

Along with *A Connecticut Yankee,* this book makes its primary appeal as a novel of ideas; like Aldous Huxley's *After Many a Summer Dies the Swan,* it combines extended philosophical dialogues with biting satire, the former passages supplying the fund of ideas, and the latter passages applying them in action. Clemens makes vituperative attacks on the sham pretense and criminal injustice of an aristocracy. He adds that the trouble is self-perpetuating, since any individual man would be a fool not to benefit from the crime if he were born into it. The only solution is for an entire nation to join together in abolishing the system. Particularly in the boardinghouse scenes, this exploration of ideas takes on a symbolic character, as when the Viscount says " 'Well, here in this very house is a republic where all are free and equal, if men are free and equal anywhere in the earth; therefore, I have arrived at the place I started to find, and I am a man among men, and on the strictest equality possible to men, no doubt.' "

∽§ §∾

In a preface to *Those Extraordinary Twins* Clemens calls himself a "jack-leg" novelist as he relates the history of this work. He began it as a "six-page tale," not really knowing where it would lead him. "But as it is a tale which [the author] is not acquainted with and can only find out what it is by listening as it goes along telling itself, it is more than apt to go on and on and on till it spreads itself into a book." When this tale had done so, he knew it had a grievous fault, but he did not discover what it was for a long time. He had combined a farce and a tragedy. We can see this peculiar blend of elements in other books—particularly in *A Connecticut Yankee*—but in no other work are the contrasts so violent. When Twain perceived the contradiction, he cut out the farce, *Those Extraordinary Twins*, which had been the nucleus idea, and published it as a separate story following *Pudd'nhead Wilson*, the "tragic" novel which grew out of the comic beginning.

In the latter, Roxana, a slave with only one-sixteenth Negro blood, bears an illegitimate son, Valet de Chambre, by a member of the local Virginia aristocracy of Dawson's Landing, Missouri. On the same day, her white mistress dies in childbirth, bringing forth a nearly identical boy, Thomas à Becket Driscoll. Roxana nurses and rears the two boys, switching them about as infants to forestall the possibility of her own son's being sold down the river as a slave. This is the same kind of reversal of roles as Clemens used in *The Prince and the Pauper,* with the distinction that the two boys are exchanged as infants and thus are not conscious of playing a false role. This book is a further demonstration of environmental conditioning, since, when the exchange is revealed after the boys have become adults, the rightful white heir finds it nearly impossible to renounce his Negro speech and cringing airs, just as King Arthur in *A Connecticut Yankee* had difficulty in counterfeiting a slave's mannerisms.

Roxy's son, now called Thomas, is adopted by his supposed uncle Judge York Leicester Driscoll after his supposed father's death. He grows up as a gambling wastrel who makes systematic thieving raids on his neighbors to pay off his St. Louis debts. At a particularly tight spot in his career, Roxy returns from her interim career as chambermaid on steamboats; penniless and exhausted, she blackmails him with the knowledge that it is Chambers, the supposed slave he has beaten and humiliated all his life, who is the real heir to Judge Driscoll's fortune.

A titled pair of Italian twins shows up at the Landing to be courted and honored by the local gentry. Although the lionizing of Counts Luigi and Angelo Capello represents the fawning of the sham Virginia aristocracy, the friendship between the visitors and Pudd'nhead Wilson is more a matter of natural aristocracy. Mr. Wilson is a loveable and mild lawyer who was stigmatized on his first arrival at the village as a numskull. He had simply remarked that if he owned half of a barking dog, he would kill his half; this joke is misunderstood by the residents who haven't the sense of humor to appreciate the remark. This is all the more evident in the sequel, *Those Extraordinary Twins*, in which the same townspeople literally do hang half of a pair of Siamese twins! Although Pudd'nhead has never been able to live down his sobriquet despite his great sagacity and goodness, the twins find pleasure in his company. He is soon given an opportunity to show his gratitude in defending Luigi, whom Tom sues for kicking him off the stage at a meeting of the "Sons of Liberty," an anti-temperance society. Even though Tom wins the case against Pudd'nhead, Judge Driscoll is deeply stirred by his "son's" abandonment of the Virginia gentleman's code in resorting to law, and challenges Luigi to a duel.

Although reinstated in the Judge's favor, Tom cannot make good secret gambling debts which, if revealed, would finally and absolutely cut him off from the Judge. Roxy, with profound but misguided motherly solicitude, suggests that Tom sell her into slavery (even though she is a free Negro) in order to pay his debts, and buy her back within a year. Because he is shamed at selling his mother at all, Tom sends her "down the river," a much crueler fate than if he sold her in Missouri where slaves were treated more humanely. Roxy escapes from her sadistic overseer and confronts Tom with the inflexible demand that he go to Judge Driscoll, confess that he has sold his mother down the river, and request the money to buy her back so that she will no longer be chased. Tom goes to the Judge, but decides to steal the money instead. Disguised as a woman, he creeps into the Judge's room only to awaken his benefactor, whereupon he stabs the Judge with an Indian knife he has stolen from the Capellos many years earlier.

Since the Capellos are the first arrivals at the scene of the crime, and since their long-lost knife is clearly the murder weapon, they are accused of the crime. Their motive is clear, for Judge Driscoll has opposed them in an election campaign, and there is a public enmity between him and the twins. Only at the last minute, by a brilliant display of detective ratiocination in the courtroom, is Pudd'nhead Wilson able to demonstrate that Tom is the real murderer, and that he is indeed not Tom at all, but Chambers, the slave son of Roxy. This is all managed by means of fingerprints, which "Pudd'nhead" has zealously collected for many years, and for which he has been labelled a harmless idiot.

It is a neatly managed, swiftly moving book, full of suspense and human interest. The character of Roxy is a powerful and admirable one, reminiscent of Dickens at his best. To be sure, others among the characters are a bit overdrawn—Tom's unfailing cruelty and meanness are not convincing and many of the characters suffer from moral over-simplification of a sort that was evident in some of the historical novels.

But the simplification has an aesthetic function here; like *The American Claimant,* the book must be read as in some way symbolic—indeed, almost as a fantasy—in order to be appreciated for what it does. For example, in the scenes where Roxy reveals to Tom that he is Negro, and where she confronts him after he has sold her down the river, there is a kind of symbolic vindictiveness about her manner, as if she were speaking for the race on some awful *dies irae*. And Tom's response is obviously meant to apply to more than his own individual crisis:

'Why were niggers *and* whites made? What crime did the uncreated first nigger commit that the curse of birth was decreed for him? And why this awful difference made between white and black? . . . How hard the nigger's fate seems, this morning!—yet until last night such a thought never entered my head.'

And there is a symbolic justice in the murder of Judge Driscoll by his own supposed son, who is in reality the product of the Virginia aristocracy's philandering with slave women.

The stern theme of retribution is a sign of Clemens' increasing pessimism; the epigraphs to the chapters of this volume constitute Pudd'nhead's famous calendar of bitter aphorisms such as these:

Whoever has lived long enough to find out what life is, knows how deep a debt of gratitude we owe to Adam, the first great benefactor of our race. He brought death into the world.

When I reflect upon the number of disagreeable people who I know have gone to a better world, I am moved to lead a different life.

The detective work is marred for the modern reader, perhaps, because of the complacency with which we regard fingerprint evidence today. Clemens actually began working on the book in 1892, the year that Sir Francis Galton brought out the first widely read book on the subject; apparently the first suggestion that fingerprints be used to identify criminals was made no earlier than 1880, although Sir William Herschel claimed he had used the system for many years in India. At any rate, Clemens was certainly the first to make fictional use of the subject (which also appears in the Karl Ritter episode in *Life on the Mississippi*). Modern experts declare that there is no more clear and convincing account of the theory of fingerprints as evidence in or out of fiction than the speech of Wilson to the court in this novel.

As far as the racial theme is concerned, the question is more complicated. Clemens' friend and fellow-lecturer, G. W. Cable, had already treated similar themes in fiction, and Clemens himself was a devoted admirer of J. C. Harris's "Uncle Remus" stories; the only kind of music he appreciated very deeply was the Negro spiritual, which he sometimes sang very feelingly for his guests of an evening. To the modern liberal, however, Clemens' use of the word "nigger" and his gusty treatment of the stereotype comic characteristics such as thievery and fright would be offensive. In *Those Extraordinary Twins*, he describes a frightened Negress who "paled to chocolate, then to orange, then to amber . . . ." This would simply be considered bad taste today, but standards were different then. In essential attitude, Clemens felt that slavery was a barbarously inhuman crime, and he said so repeatedly and openly. He sponsored a Negro student at Yale. And in this novel, his treatment of Roxy and Tom is honest, sympathetic, and direct. He does not soft-pedal the ignorance, superstition, or moral shortcomings of his Negro characters, but he puts the blame for these shortcomings where it belongs—on the crime of slavery. In fact, Clemens says as much at the end of the book. Tom's creditors come forth when they learn that he is in reality a Negro slave, and they insist that since he is property, they have a call on him for the period before he became a murderer; both the court and Clemens approve of his being sold down the river into slavery as a fate worse than any punishment a murderer undergoes.

Those Extraordinary Twins are Counts Luigi and Angelo Capello, converted, for the farcical episode, into a creature with two heads, four arms, and but one pair of legs. Clemens apparently got the idea from a portrait of an actual pair of twins, Giovanni and Giacomo Tocci, which was published in *Scientific American* along with a description that tallies with some of the details in his story. Luigi, dark and devilish, constantly pains the fair and innocent Angelo. Luigi drinks hard liquor and smokes while Angelo swallows headache pills and suffocates. One is a free thinker, the other a Methodist well on the way to becoming a Baptist. As they prepare for bed, Luigi reads Tom Paine, while Angelo applies himself to *The Whole Duty of Man*. When Angelo's tenor soars into a missionary hymn, Luigi's bass intones a raucous secular ballad. One runs for alderman on the Democratic ticket, the other on the Whig.

The tale itself is fragmentary, since Clemens never revised the chapters so that they could stand alone separately from *Pudd'n-head Wilson*. Aside from introductory clowning, the trial scene in Chapter V, in which the twins are charged with assault for having kicked Tom at the Sons of Liberty meeting, is a comic masterpiece worthy to stand beside nearly anything else Clemens produced in this genre. The major problem of ascertaining which of the twins willed the kick is a ready-made legal tangle. Mr. Wilson's discomfiting the witnesses with unanswerable questions is also in the grand legal-comic tradition, as is the irreverent and talky witness, here represented by Aunt Patsy Cooper and Aunt Betsy Hale. The unique comic element is the judge, Mr. Justice Robinson, who knows very little law and who scorns the precedents and methods of all other courts. He deals with the law in a freewheeling manner that would be a scandal, were it not that in every case the common sense judgment is upheld over the artificial legal sophistry. In this he resembles Captain Ned Blakely of *Roughing It* who administers roughshod justice to the man who shot his Negro first mate.

Scenes follow in which the twins lecture alternately to Democratic and Whig assemblies, and temperance and anti-temperance societies, depending on which one has command of the one pair of legs that week. Luigi fights the duel with Judge Driscoll, which is abruptly ended at midnight by the wounded Angelo, who at that moment has rightful command over the legs. His revenge occurs when he is totally immersed in baptism, and Luigi, the freethinker, is forced to undergo the ceremony too. The book ends violently. Luigi has been elected to office as alderman, but Angelo is not permitted to sit at the meetings. Thus it is decided that Luigi, who delays the functions of government by this dilemma, must be hanged. This reminds us that Clemens in an earlier version disposed of five characters in succession by having them accidentally drowned in the same well. Obviously he was as innocent of artistic conscience as a tadpole.

Clemens had heretofore presented many cases of a reversal of roles—between a king and a slave in *Connecticut Yankee*, between a prince and a pauper, and between a slave and a master in the volume that is a Siamese twin to this one. But never before had he attempted to fuse such markedly opposing elements in the same person. It is almost as if the extravagance of the comedy in this book were a sign that Clemens had carried this device as far as it could go aesthetically for him. This is the last of his major

works which attempts such a device, aside from abortive unpublished manuscripts.

✎§ §✍

Clemens' American novels are all involved with a kind of flam-
boyance—Congressional corruption, sordid murder, and the profound sorrows of slaves, interlarded with the sledge-hammer humor
of freak twins and near-maniacs. The short stories bear these
marks, in addition to characteristics shared with the autobiographical, travel, and historical writings.

Aside from the distinctly moral tales, which we shall consider in
the closing chapter, the pieces of highest quality may easily be
the short humorous bits. "Mrs. McWilliams and the Lightning,"
"The Experience of the McWilliamses with the Membranous
Croup," and "The McWilliamses and the Burglar Alarm" are
obviously disguised treatments of Clemens' family life, with the
patient, rational male at the mercy of a beloved but distraught
wife's feminine intuitions and fears. In "Playing the Courier,"
"The Canvasser's Tale," and "Political Economy," the absent-
minded husband is portrayed at a hilarious disadvantage. The
latter two, which deal with traveling salesmen who peddle echoes
and lightning rods, share with "My Watch" the classic basis
of humor dealing with life's little exasperations as embodied in
salespersons. "Journalism in Tennessee" and "How I Edited an
Agricultural Paper" are examples of nearly hysterically exaggerated "tall-tale" humor.

Satire on bureaucracy predominates in "The Facts in the Great
Beef Contract," "The Man Who Put Up at Gadsby's" (*A Tramp
Abroad*), "Two Little Tales," and "The Belated Russian Pass-
port," which also deals heavily in melodrama.

From his earliest newspaper work, Clemens was well-trained in
the art of burlesque and parody, which finds brilliant expression
in "The Story of the Bad Little Boy" and "The Story of the Good
Little Boy," wicked distortions of the syrupy but cruel Sunday
School literature of Clemens' youth. He plays with the familiar
problem of the experiential contradictions of the pretty theory of
reward and punishment. "Some Learned Fables for Old Boys and
Girls" is a less successful satire in which a group of insects on a
scientific expedition are used to reflect discredit on both the
human race and its dogmatic display of learning. "A Medieval Romance" is a *reductio ad absurdum* of narrative methods of the

middle ages; he leads his characters into a hopeless tangle based on a kind of Shakespearian sexual masquerade. Then he cheerfully abandons his characters at the height of their confusion, as he also does in "A Story Without an End" from *Following the Equator*. In the latter, his hero is seated in a wagon without any pants on, in a situation that urgently requires him to relinquish the lap robe to a bevy of proper matrons. Some of the most insistent and pointed burlesque was aimed at detective literature, despite his own success in *Pudd'nhead Wilson*. "The Stolen White Elephant" is a brutal attack on the detectives' pretensions to certainty, as is "A Double-Barreled Detective Story," which makes mincemeat of Sherlock Holmes himself.

Another classic story type is joshed in "A Ghost Story," in which the ghost of the Cardiff Giant is informed that his body is only a fake plaster cast, and in "A Curious Dream," an exposure of the condition of an unkempt cemetery.

The romantic love story is handled as gently as a steer in a slaughterhouse in two violent burlesques, "The Loves of Alonzo Fitz Clarence and Rosannah Ethelton" and "The Esquimau Maiden's Romance." Alonzo and Rosannah undergo all the fiendish tortures of a long-distance telephone courtship and marriage long before such a situation was physically possible. Lasca, the maiden from the frozen north, attracts just the fiance she most desires; her father, the richest man in the area, showers her lavishly with all twenty-two of his iron fishhooks just to show off his wealth. When one of the hooks is missing, her fiance is executed on suspicion of theft. After her suitor has perished on a floating ice floe, she gives her hair its yearly combing and discovers the missing fishhook.

"A Curious Experience" and "The Death Disk" are belabored and ineffective historical romances. The former is a suspense piece about a boy who is mistaken for a Confederate spy in a Union Army camp. The latter is a sentimental melodrama about an Army daughter who unwittingly nearly condemns her father to death for excessive heroism under Cromwell.

Another group of tales can best be treated as "gimmick" stories, some with the familiar O. Henry twist that suddenly destroys the reader's carefully nurtured expectations. "Luck" details the career of an incompetent British officer who mounts to brilliant heights of fame on pure chance. In "The Californian's Tale" Clemens uses a formula which is the reverse of Saki's "The Open Window." A miner regales a visitor with stories of his young bride who is to return very shortly; at the end of the piece, we learn she has been dead nineteen years. We have already noted, of course, that *Life on the Mississippi* contains a number of such yarns, and *Following the Equator* has its share too. The most elaborate one outside these volumes is "The £1,000,000 Bank Note," in which a San Francisco mining clerk is set loose in London with one gargantuan piece of currency, simply to see how people treat him.

"The Legend of the Capitoline Venus" and "Is He Living or Is He Dead?" concern two artistic hoaxes. In one of these an unsaleable modern statue is damaged and buried for a time, bringing a huge price after its "discovery" as an ancient statue. The other story concerns an artist who is able to sell an immense number of paintings only after it is announced (falsely) that he is dead. In these pieces, Clemens satirizes the reverence for antiquity and for dead artists that characterizes our art criticism even today.

It may be a highly primitive or else a cultivated, sophisticated taste that delights in extravagance of effect, but for those who are amused by it, "Cannibalism in the Cars" and "The Invalid's Story" are incomparable. It is only accidental that both are railroad tales. The former tale deals with a group of men marooned in a snow storm who fastidiously and formally elect the fellow candidates for breakfast, dinner, and supper. The invalid of the second story is a narrator whose health has been shattered by a trip in a baggage car. He is escorting a pine box, supposedly containing the body of a boyhood friend, but actually containing rifles. The odor of the box of limburger cheese which has been placed on top of the pine box inspires the narrator and the baggage man to superhuman efforts of forbearance and endurance as the car gets hotter and hotter. As the penetrating, nauseating odor mounts, Clemens rises to the heights of comic invention.

In stories about animals, Clemens is often superior, running from the early and celebrated jumping frog through "Tom Quartz," the marvelous cat of *Roughing It* to "What Stumped the Blue Jays" of *A Tramp Abroad*. On the other hand, his unsuccessful animal stories, "A Dog's Tale" and "A Horse's Tale," are perhaps inferior because they were requested as object lessons against vivisection and bullfighting; it is no wonder that Clemens was unsuccessful in trying to write the sort of thing that he excoriated so heartily and hearteningly in his burlesques on Sunday School literature!

At the opposite extreme is the touching chronicle of Aunt Rachel as related in "A True Story," one of Clemens' best short pieces. One evening at Quarry Farm, the cook, Auntie Cord, related to the Clemens family her history as a slave, the separation of her family, and the accidental reunion with her youngest son during the Civil War. Clemens has transcribed the narration simply and directly in a dialect that hits a golden mean between realism and literary invention. It demonstrates his great mastery of the technique of colloquial anecdote rendered at a plane of high artistic quality.

The most appealing quality of Clemens' American novels and tales is the panoramic breadth of material. With Roxy and Aunt Rachel, Thomas à Becket Driscoll and Valet de Chambre, we have admirable portraits of slave experience in Virginia, Arkansas, and Missouri, along with the complicated problems of miscegenation. We are taken to mining camps in the West, and catch glimpses of San Francisco opulence and culture. In *Pudd'nhead Wilson, Those Extraordinary Twins,* and the early sections of *The Gilded Age*, Clemens gives us a picture in depth of small-town Missouri life before the Civil War, full of political rallies, temperance meetings, gossip, and social functions. The wide range of types includes the town drunkard, kindly old widows, starry-eyed maidens, gambling wastrels, river and steamboat characters, and ex-Virginia aristocrats. As we move on in time, we find in the bulk of *The Gilded Age* an indictment of Reconstruction government in Washington, full of fantastic hypocrisy and corruption; in the portrait of the Bolton family, we also see how the upper middle class suffered from the speculation and the boom-and-bust economy which they too swallowed whole hog. *The American Claimant* is an extended essay on equalitarianism in which a contemporary British aristocrat makes a kind of "Connecticut Yankee" voyage in reverse, learning at first hand from boardinghouse philosophers lessons in American democracy.

7

✌ BOY LITERATURE

CLEMENS' American reputation is based firmly on the unparalleled achievement of his books about boys. With or without the approval of professional and academic critics, the books would have held the secure place in the heart of the reading public that they continue to occupy. Clemens himself called *Tom Sawyer* a "hymn" to boyhood, and it is with a kind of reverent awe that most readers experience the clarity, skill, and naturalness of this account of how it felt to grow up in a Missouri river town.

The Adventures of Tom Sawyer (1876) is a delightful book because, as Kenneth S. Lynn has remarked, it confirms the profoundest wishes of the heart. Even though it deals with grave-robbers, slow starvation, cruelty, and brutality, it ultimately exonerates the values of the small town in which Clemens' generation grew up, and, by extension, the small town that each of us carries in his memory if only as a kind of historic heritage. *Adventures of Huckleberry Finn* (1885) is a sequel that soared even higher than its predecessor. It has been the subject of the most extravagant praise and the most detailed critical analysis of all Clemens' books because it is certainly one of the half-dozen greatest books America has ever produced. It is superior to *Tom Sawyer* because it is a more serious and disturbing view of the same small town; by now the violence and brutality that served a melodramatic purpose in the earlier books have been refracted through the profound moral issues of slavery and human dignity.

maybe

The sensitive and suffering Huck Finn, who floats down the Mississippi isolated on his raft with the fleeing slave Jim, serves as a conscience for an entire era and culture. And he is not reconciled to what he sees. In town after town, he undergoes traumatic revelations of human depravity that palpably sicken him. The only fault in the novel, for most readers, is the breakdown of the whole plot and theme toward the end, when Clemens seems to indulge in unnecessary clowning. But on a second glance, we shall see that even this almost universally maligned ending has its justification. Aside from this problem, the book is a triumph, whether considered from the point of view of historical, social, and moral significance; style; characterization; or just plain good reading. *Tom Sawyer Abroad* (1894) and *Tom Sawyer, Detective* (1896) are the only two of his later projects involving the boys to reach print. In these cases, he is obviously using the travel book and the detective yarn, two forms that haunted his imagination, as vehicles for further adventures. The former was never satisfactorily completed, and the latter, although interesting as an involved tale of ratiocination, has neither the beauty of *Tom Sawyer* nor the profundity of *Huck Finn* to recommend it.

The composition of the major works is typical. The idea for *Tom Sawyer* was one that haunted him for a long time before this version was begun in 1873 or 1874, after which he worked on it intermittently. Since this was the first novel he attempted all alone, he was a bit fearful about the tone until Howells' enthusiastic praise calmed him. When the book finally appeared, it was an immediate success.

In the meantime, he began *Huckleberry Finn* in 1876, and then abandoned the manuscript with a half-hearted vow to burn it. He took it up again at various points, probably in 1879, 1880, and 1883; in 1880, he spoke of publishing it along with *The Prince and the Pauper* in one volume, but his wife adamantly refused to have one of her favorite tales besmirched by appearing along with the adventures of a boy-tramp. All the evidence points to the assumption that Clemens himself hardly realized this was to become his greatest book.

❧ ❧

Clemens glides into his most endearing tone in the quiet opening chapters of *Tom Sawyer*. The child struggles to accommodate his boy-nature to the standards of the harassed but tender-hearted Aunt Polly, who is supported gently by Mary. Brother Sid is the

"I AM THE LATE DAUPHIN."

"PAP."

COL. GRANGERFORD.

SOLID COMFORT.

Illustrations from *Huckleberry Finn*

"good boy" of the Sunday School manuals, who sanctimoniously pits his subtle perceptions against Tom's inevitable "bad boy" tendencies; he is pitiless in informing against his brother for sneak swimming jaunts and the like. The whole narration is a rich harvest of early recollections; nearly all the incidents are paralleled by passages in the *Autobiography*. Tom is drawn from Clemens himself and two friends, John Briggs and Will Bowen. Jane Clemens' traits are gathered into Aunt Polly, and brother Henry's into Sid. Injun Joe, the members of Tom's gang, Becky Thatcher, the caves, the island—all the details are based on Clemens' boyhood in Hannibal.

The intense honesty to the feel of experience in these passages is undoubtedly what led Hemingway (who is a stickler for just this sort of honesty in his own works) to praise Mark Twain as extravagantly as he did. Whether Hemingway learned this exclusively from Twain is not easy to determine, but the two writers certainly share a genius for paring away the inessential and for presenting the bare core of experience with devastating authenticity. The first evidence of this classically economical style is in the arrival of Ben Rogers during the famous whitewashing incident of Chapter II:

> As he drew nearer, he slackened speed, took the middle of the street, leaned far over to starboard and rounded to ponderously and with laborious pomp and circumstance—for he was personating the *Big Missouri,* and considered himself to be drawing nine feet of water. He was boat and captain and engine-bells combined, so he had to imagine himself standing on his own hurricane-deck giving orders and executing them. . . .

In these and ensuing sentences, all the pure essentials of child imagination are presented with an authority and simplicity that make the writing incomparable.

Tom goes his merry way, beating up the neatly dressed new boy in town and alternately showing off for and mooning over the new girl, Becky Thatcher. Chapters IV and V are a climax of this early section in their genial and tender treatment of Sunday School and Church services; the style of these passages is at its impeccable best, so that the writing seems to sing. It is a miracle of tone that encompasses the hypocritical, pompous airs of the adults, Tom's fraudulent scheming to gain the prize Bible, and the neatly arranged accident whereby the pinchbug tortures the dog into breaking up the sermon. There is a gentle, timeless beauty about the chapters, as if each harsh motive or jarring conflict were seen

in the hazy forest light of genial recollection—a light that endears
and softens reality without falsifying one detail.

Chapter VI introduces Huck, the "town pariah," drawn after
Tom Blankenship, a boyhood companion. Son of an ignorant,
bestial drunk, he represents all that is untamed and untamable.

> Huckleberry came and went, at his own free will. He slept on door-
> steps in fine weather and in empty hogsheads in wet; he did not
> have to go to school or to church, or call any being master or obey
> anybody; he could go fishing or swimming when and where he
> chose, and stay as long as it suited him; nobody forbade him to
> fight; he could sit up as late as he pleased; he was always the first
> boy that went barefoot in the spring and the last to resume leather
> in the fall; he never had to wash, nor put on clean clothes; he
> could swear wonderfully. In a word, everything that goes to make
> life precious, that boy had. So thought every harassed, hampered,
> respectable boy in St. Petersburg.

He is to Tom what Tom is to Sid. By no means as clever or articulate as Tom, he also has less courage, especially in matters that
call for a civilized resourcefulness. He exists on the very fringe
of organized society and wants no truck with the inhabitants of
even the smallest of hamlets. Regularity stifles him to such a
degree that he complains, during a sojourn with Widow Douglas,
that the certainty of knowing in advance what one will eat and
when one will eat it would kill him.

After Tom becomes "engaged" to Becky, he lights out with
Huck to a graveyard for a midnight incantation over a dead cat,
in an effort to remove warts. The copious folk superstition revealed in these books is closely related, psychologically, to the
unfounded convictions of overwhelming personal guilt with which
the boys are afflicted. Both superstition and guilt are based on
fear and ignorance: in the case of superstition, one substitutes a
magic cause and effect relationship in order to control or placate
exterior forces, whereas guilt is a form of fear about interior forces
within the individual which he does not understand. Although the
mature Clemens rejected superstition and, at least in a symbolic
sense, murdered his conscience in "The Facts Concerning a Recent
Carnival of Crime in Connecticut," he nevertheless knew how
powerfully related the two forces were in the experience of a boy.
This is why Huck and Tom are interrupted in their ritual by
three sinister figures who are to plunge the boys into an orgy of
guilt feelings.

Muff Potter and Injun Joe have been hired by Dr. Robinson to dig up the newly buried body of Hoss Williams over which the boys were to have performed their ceremony. As the terrified children look on, Injun Joe tries to blackmail the doctor, and in the ensuing argument, Joe stabs Dr. Robinson to death. He then rouses the drunken Muff Potter and convinces him it was he who killed the doctor. The boys are so horrified at what they have seen—and at what Joe would do to them if they attempted to exonerate Muff—that they swear a blood oath never to reveal the crime. Then, neatly enough, what began as superstition and blended into guilt at seeing injustice done, turns again to superstition as their oath is climaxed by seeing a dog howl at the sleeping Muff, a sure sign he is to die for the crime he did not commit. Next day the boys also see Joe calmly testify to Muff's guilt. Tom's mental anguish is so deep that he talks in his sleep, and even feigns toothache in order to tie up his jaws and thereby prevent the ever-vigilant Sid from hearing his mutterings.

Clemens then eases up on the melodrama by providing a different, and nearly idyllic, variation on the theme of guilt. Tom, Huck, and Joe Harper run away to Jackson's Island to play pirate. Throughout these volumes, it is Tom who has read the glamorous literature of romance—first it is Robin Hood, then pirates, then robbers, culminating in *Huckleberry Finn*, with literal allusions to the supremely deluded idealist, Don Quixote. He organizes his playmates into gangs to pursue ruinous dreams of glory) This time the boys are hardly established in their island hideaway before they begin to feel guilty for running away and for stealing ham and bacon as provisions. The guilt is augmented—again, in close relation to superstition—by their seeing the steamboat that fires across the water and launches loaves of bread filled with quicksilver in order to recover their supposedly drowned bodies.

Tom's thirst for heroic grandeur makes him the cohesive force that keeps the incipiently mutinous gang together. His resourcefulness as a leader is demonstrated in his trip back to St. Petersburg one evening. He spies on his mourning family who are visited by Mrs. Harper, just as he and Huck accidentally spied on the murder of Dr. Robinson. We shall see as we go along that the repetition of such devices as these spying episodes is in reality what holds these books together much more effectively than plot. We shall call such organization a "theme and variations" structure, since it is very close to musical use of themes. Again and again Tom wants to jump out from under the bed and reveal himself, much as he and Huck must have felt suppressed impulses to prevent the doctor's murder. But when he hears that a funeral service is to be held on Sunday morning, his sense of showmanship demands that he keep the secret until the three "dead" boys can dramatically walk in on their own funeral. This situation of being thought dead is another of the organizational themes of these books.)

The third guilt cycle is based on the consequences of Tom's return. He cannot resist telling Aunt Polly in great detail about all he saw the evening he was under the bed, as if he had dreamed it all. She later discovers he was lying, which leads to an emotional scene and a touching reconciliation. Exactly the same cycle occurs, with even greater intensity, in Tom's relation with Becky. Immediately on his return to school, he sports and splashes around in his new-found glory, ignoring Becky and paying court to Amy Lawrence, a former sweetheart, in order to stoke Becky's emotional fires. She retaliates by favoring Alfred Temple, who is so intoxicated by her attention that he purposely spills ink on Tom's spelling lesson for the day. Becky, dejected and tearful, happens upon an anatomy book that the teacher usually keeps carefully hidden, and is absorbed in a plate representing a naked human figure when Tom comes along. She accidentally rips the page in her struggle to keep Tom from seeing what she is looking at. Again we see the "theme and variations" structure in that we now have two damaged books to account for. Tom is punished early in the afternoon for the spelling book, and later pretends it was he who tore the anatomy book, thus receiving a second, and very hefty, beating. But this, of course, endears him to Becky.

By the time the murder trial occurs, Tom has broken down and told the defense lawyer what he and Huck saw and overheard in the graveyard. They had nursed their guilt by giving Muff tobacco and various comforting tidbits through the jail window, just as Clemens himself gave matches to a tramp in Hannibal. But this substitute expiation was not enough to soothe Tom's conscience, so he broke his oath to Huck. When Injun Joe's guilt is revealed in the courtroom, he leaps through a window and escapes.

In Chapter XXI we encounter a variation on the Sunday School and Church services in a treatment of "Examination Day" at school; Clemens regales his readers with choice examples of schoolgirl compositions, a device he is to repeat in *Huckleberry Finn*. Tom's brief membership in the Cadets of Temperance and his measles are adaptations of experiences described in the *Autobiography*.

Here we enter on a new cycle which is compounded of the now-familiar elements of superstition, guilt, spying, and violence when Tom and Huck begin an ineffectual treasure-digging expedition. After many false starts, they end up on the second floor of a haunted house, where they overhear Injun Joe, now disguised as a deaf and dumb Spaniard, plotting with a companion to get his "revenge" before they flee with their hidden treasure. Thus in the third "eavesdropping" incident, Tom and Huck ironically gain a lead on a treasure without even digging. Tom reasons that Joe may be staying at a second-rate temperance hotel, and he puts Huck on a schedule of spying there. In the meantime, Tom himself goes off on a picnic to the caves which has long been promised by Becky's parents. Just as the lights of the ferryboat returning with the picnickers appear in town, Huck is spying on Injun Joe, and follows him and his companion out of town. They stop outside the Widow Douglas's where Huck hears Joe plotting to slit her nose and notch her ears in payment for an old grudge against her husband. He runs to inform the Welshman, Jones, and his sons, who scare off Joe and his companion by shots.

It is only the next morning at church that Tom's and Becky's people learn that they did not return from the picnic, but are presumably lost in the cave. This turns out to be another variation on a familiar theme, because again Tom was attempting to show off as an intrepid hero when he led Becky into an unexplored portion of the cave. His subsequent guilt is also the familiar consequence. By accident, the cave is also the hiding place of Injun Joe, whom Tom narrowly escapes in one of his meandering explorations. He and Becky eventually find their way out at a hitherto unknown passage five miles away from the entrance to the cave. When the children return, Judge Thatcher seals up the entrance to the cave to avoid future tragedies, but after his recovery, Tom reveals that Injun Joe was inside. The body is discovered at the entrance, where he died in a pathetic attempt to dig his way out. Tom and Huck then re-enter the cave by Tom's rear entrance and dig out Injun Joe's treasure of $1200. Tom melodramatically reveals the new wealth at a most telling moment, as is his habit—at a celebration at the Widow's to honor Huck for saving her from mutilation.

The book ends with Tom's giving Sid a good, healthy cuffing, and with his wallowing in his own heroic grandeur for saving Becky and gaining the fortune. Huck is taken in by the Widow Douglas and bears the rigors of cleanliness, prayers, regularity, and gentility for just three weeks, before he lights out for the woods and the docks. Tom reconciles the various themes in his plan for Huck to become a member of his new midnight gang of robbers, which will be bullier than Robin Hood or pirates—only on the provision that Huck will try to bear up at the Widow Douglas's and face the additional horrors of school.

We have, thus, a book that gives a genial and warmhearted backward glance at boyhood in Missouri, one that deals in typical children's moral dilemmas like clandestine swimming, smoking, running away from home, disliking church, and torturing animals. To this is added the high melodrama and violence of grave-robbing, murder, theft, mutilation, and starvation. This first set of elements is genuine; it is the basis of the book's wide fame because the emotional tone of the narration is so gentle, forgiving, and understanding. The violent elements have an obvious sensational value, but if this were all they had, then the book would consist of two unrelated sets of elements. Actually, the sensational incidents are a kind of intensified projection of the childhood moral dilemmas, like magnified shadows on a wall that take on a hallucinatory quality. Common to both these sets of elements is the moral significance inherent in the repeated situations involving superstition, guilt, spying, suffering, and reconciliation.

In the contrast between the bragging, bullying, romantically ingenious and inventive Tom and the uncombed, unshod unregenerate child of the woods and the docks as represented by Huck, we have a dichotomy that must represent two very profound aspects of Clemens' own nature. We have already noticed in many books his propensity for dealing with pseudonymous personalities, split natures, twins, and contrasting pairs. Tom represents Clemens' insatiable egotism, his love of fame, money, attention, and glory. His biographer notes that even as an old and sick man, he walked the long way around in order to go through a hotel lobby where people would stare and whisper at his unusual clothes, rather than go quietly down by the back way. Huck, on the other hand, embodies his self-confessed laziness, love of profanity, billiards, and little-boy naughtinesses. In the moral sphere, both Tom and Huck pay plentifully for their natural desires and impulses, and to this degree, the novel is a serious and adult book as Clemens maintains it was meant to be in his preface.

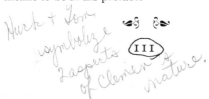

Huck + Tom
symbolize
2 aspects
of Clemens + nature.

❧ ❦

⟨III⟩

Mark Twain

Although *Huckleberry Finn* is a sequel to *Tom Sawyer* and deals with many of the same preoccupations(on the first page the reader notes with a rush of pleasure that this narrative is in the first person. Because Huck tells his story himself, the stylistic richness is immeasurably deepened by the rhythms, intonations, and choice of words of this magnificent child) He takes up the story during his second sojourn with the Widow Douglas, which he undertook in order to be a member of Tom's gang. When they have to raid a Sunday School picnic and pretend that they have found Spanish merchants, Arabs, elephants, camels, and diamonds, Huck has had enough. Tom, in his deluded pursuit of swashbuckling glory, is true to his literary model, Don Quixote; Huck, without reading the book, naturally takes the role of skeptical Sancho Panza. In this volume his pragmatism comes to the fore as a major character trait. When he hears about Aladdin's magic lamp, he tries to rouse a genie himself; he tries to pray, but with no success:

> I set down one time back in the woods, and had a long think about it. I says to myself, if a body can get anything they pray for, why don't Deacon Winn get back the money he lost on pork? Why can't the widow get back her silver snuff-box that was stole? Why can't Miss Watson fat up? No, says I to myself, there ain't nothing in it. I went and told the widow about it, and she said the thing a body could get by praying for it was 'spiritual gifts.' This was too many for me, but she told me what she meant—I must help other people, and do everything I could for other people, and look out for them all the time, and never think about myself. This was including Miss Watson, as I took it. I went out in the woods and turned it over in my mind a long time, but I couldn't see no advantage about it—except for the other people; so at last I reckoned I wouldn't worry about it any more, but just let it go.

He decides early in the book that the kindly Widow Douglas has a different Providence in mind than the disciplinarian Miss Watson, the sister who supervises Huck's spelling lessons. And he unhesitatingly decides that if Miss Watson will be in heaven and Tom Sawyer in hell, there is no choice at all about where he will want to go.

As if he has not found these foster-parents perplexing enough, Huck's long-lost drunkard father shows up and as soon as he learns his son is rich, takes a proprietary interest in the boy, forbidding him to go to school, dress in fine clothes, or put on any airs) He takes Huck to a cabin in the woods and beats him brutally between his own bouts with delirium tremens. Aside from the beatings, Huck is on the whole happier in the woods, fishing and hunting for daily sustenance, than he was at the Widow's. In Pap's drunken monologues against a government that will not let him drink up his son's sudden wealth and that will protect free Negroes from immediate sale, Clemens gives us a rich and racy sample of frontier talk that is worth volumes of historical analysis.

When his father attempts to murder him in a fit of drunkenness, Huck perfects his plan to saw his way out of the cabin and contrive all the evidences of his own murder in order to prevent pursuit by either the Widow or Pap. Once established on Jackson's Island, where he has played pirate with Tom Sawyer, he sees the ferry again firing over the water and floating off the bread with quicksilver. His brash assurance of having fooled the town is abruptly broken when he discovers the remains of a recent campfire on the island. He finds shortly that his fellow-fugitive is Miss Watson's Negro servant Jim, who has fled to avoid being sold down the river. Once Jim is convinced Huck is not a ghost, the two become firm allies. They make themselves comfortable on the island and while away time by exploring an abandoned house floating by on the floodwaters.

Huck decides to visit St. Petersburg for news; in an incident that parallels Tom's secret visit to his home in *Tom Sawyer,* Huck dresses as a girl and learns from Mrs. Loftus, who sees through the disguise, but not far enough to identify him, that various people in town blame Jim for the murder of Huck, now that their suspicion of Pap has let up. In fact, Mr. Loftus means to leave soon for the island in order to hunt Jim down for the reward money. Huck races back to the island; the two fugitives load all their gear on a raft and set out down the river in a hurry. From here on, the book itself follows the sinuous, shifting current of the Mississippi southward during its spring rise, as it redoubles upon itself in thematic repetitions and variations.

South of St. Louis, Huck and Jim come upon the wreck of the steamboat *Walter Scott.* Although Jim would rather "leave blame' well alone," Huck wants to board the wreck, remembering how gloriously Tom would avail himself of this romantic adventure, like Columbus discovering Kingdom Come, says Huck. Once aboard, they run upon three desperadoes, two of whom are about to murder the third for treachery. As Huck listens to their deliberations, we remember how he and Tom overheard the scenes in the graveyard and in the haunted house.

The melodrama runs as high as the river when Jim and Huck find that their own raft has torn loose, and the desperadoes are about to enter their skiff. Only the greed of the robbers, who go back to frisk their abandoned accomplice, provides Huck and Jim with a chance to escape on the robbers' skiff. With a familiar kind of poetic justice, all three criminals are subjected to the fate they had reserved for one—the ship looses from the snag and floats down the river, sinking all the time. Huck makes heroic efforts to get help, but to no avail.

The random goods that the fugitives gain from the steamboat recall the goods they got from the floating house; in a sense, the river provides for them in a motherly way. But it can also show a cruel side, as when Huck in the canoe and Jim on the raft are separated in the fog; hardly do they find each other when the gray evening so confounds visibility that the raft is struck by a steamboat, and they are separated again.

Before this happens, Huck plays a joke on Jim, recalling the time he had put a dead rattlesnake in Jim's blanket on Jackson's Island, only to have Jim bitten by the snake's mate. This time, after fifteen minutes of wrestling with his conscience, he humbles himself to Jim, an act unprecedented in his background. In the next chapter, the second great moral crisis occurs, in which Huck must violate his upbringing even more radically. They have been watching for Cairo, Illinois, and the confluence of the Ohio River, where Jim can go North to gain freedom. For the first time Huck realizes he has helped a runaway slave, and, by the code in which he was reared, he is stealing another man's property—and when Jim makes enough money to buy or steal away his wife and children, that will only compound the evil. But Huck's pragmatic morality sees him through the dilemma, because he judges that if he feels bad about helping a runaway slave, he'd feel just as bad after he turned him in. "Well, then, says I, what's the use you learning to do right when it's troublesome to do right and ain't no trouble to do wrong, and the wages is just the same? I was stuck. I couldn't answer that. So I reckoned I wouldn't bother no more about it, but after this always do whichever come handiest at the time."

As a result of the second separation, Huck encounters the first of a series of shore adventures that give us one of the most comprehensive surveys of mid-American society of that day. The Grangerford home at which Huck is suspiciously received in the dead of night represents the affluent and naturally "aristocratic" planter class. In the rich description of the furnishings of the home and the customs of the household—ending with the bloody feud that decimates a family—there is an unspoken assumption that by and large ante-bellum plantation culture is just one step removed from the frontier. This is a society in which high civilization only fitfully shines through the brutality and crudity of a raw living arrangement. In the twenty years that have elapsed since Clemens joined a Confederate volunteer group, his attitude toward the South has obviously changed. Huck's observations throughout this episode show a mounting exasperation at a group who carry their rifles into church with them in order to hear a sermon on brotherly love; the exasperation has turned to sickened disgust at the close of the episode with the wholesale butchery of the Grangerford men at the steamboat landing by the Shepherdsons. It is Huck who has the repugnant duty to pull from the river the body of his old buddy Buck, and his refusal to comment on his feelings is one of the most touchingly eloquent passages in the book.

The opening of Chapter XIX provides, in the quiet intermezzo describing the uneventful raft life that the naked Huck and Jim resume, one of the most shimmeringly beautiful passages in all of Clemens' writings.

As Huck explores a side-stream, he is appropriated by a pair of scoundrels fleeing the vengeance of two enraged communities; the Duke of Bridgewater and the Dauphin of France, as the men style themselves, are two of the most consummate rascals ever portrayed in literature, short of Falstaff himself. Like the "Celebrated Jumping Frog," the incidents involving the Duke and the Dauphin represent the apotheosis of one strain of Southwestern humor. There is a long tradition of sketches of the traveling confidence-man who fleeces the yokels at camp meetings, horse-tradings, and fake shows. This pair share between them most of the characteristics of the traditional figures, but are nevertheless an integral part of the theme of this novel. The two take over the raft immediately, retaining Huck and Jim as scraping and obsequious servants. Almost before we have our bearings, the King has bilked a Pokeville camp meeting of $87.75 and the Duke has taken a printing establishment for $9.50. But this is just warming up for the $465 they draw at another little Arkansas town for three performances of the obscene "Royal Nonesuch," wisely fleeing the town just after they collect tickets for the third performance.

While waiting for the performance, Huck has had a view of a

typical small river town and its inhabitants, which must be added to the Grangerford episode for a full view of the river culture. He reveals a depressing situation—mud streets, junk heaps, run-down houses, pigs wallowing in the mire, loafers haggling over a chaw —laziness is compounded with filth, brutality, cowardice, ignorance, and vulgarity. As always, however, it is Huck's perceptive and pragmatic consciousness that selects the telling details. As Boggs, the town drunkard, threatens Colonel Sherburn, who, in exasperation, shoots down the braggart in broad daylight on the main street, Huck does not commit himself to one side or the other. If he directly condemns any element in the situation, it is the crowd of onlookers. Huck is the only one who notes the cruelty of placing a heavy Bible on the chest of the dying Boggs. His revulsion from the crowd is most explicit as he describes their morbid curiosity in going over the scene of the shooting and crowding around the dying man. He follows the lynch mob as it approaches Colonel Sherburn's house, and listens as the Colonel harangues them from the roof of his porch. In this speech, the Colonel's explicit condemnation of Southern mob violence—and Northern cowardice as well—shows many parallels to "suppressed" material written for *Life on the Mississippi* which appeared for the first time in the edition of Edward Wagenknecht in 1944.

Then Huck relieves the tension by a rollicking session at a local circus. Again the "theme and variations" structure is evident when Huck is totally fooled by a comic drunk in the audience who turns out to be a skillful bareback rider in the circus; he is in the same position as the audiences whom the Duke and King gull with the "Royal Nonesuch."

The crowning achievement of the King and the Duke is the fleecing of the Wilks girls. On the prowl for new devilment, the King finds out that the three young women, having lost their uncle Peter the preceding day, are expecting his English brothers— Harvey, a preacher, and William, a deaf-mute—to settle the disposition of Peter Wilks' estate. When the King has found out all he needs to know from a talkative young neighbor, he arrives posing as the preacher, with the Duke playing the deaf and dumb brother. They completely hoodwink the family and the town, with the exception of the learned Dr. Robinson who immediately sees through the King's shoddy accent and fake Greek. Huck's disapproval of the pair of charlatans finally finds its expression in action—which he has not dared heretofore—when he steals the $6,000 that the scoundrels have taken from the girls; in the sud-

den emergency, he is forced to cram the sack into Peter's coffin.

After one of Clemens' typically comic funerals, the actual heirs show up on the day that the house and furnishings are to be auctioned; Dr. Robinson and lawyer Levi Bell conduct an investigation to find out which is the genuine pair of heirs and to lynch the pretenders. It eventually centers on the question of the tattoo marks on the corpse's chest. During a crashing thunderstorm, the body is dug up, but before anyone can investigate the tattoo, the bag of gold is found in the coffin, and the crowd is so flabbergasted that Huck manages to run off and the King and the Duke follow shortly. When they all reach the raft, there is a bitter argument about who was deserting whom, an argument which parallels the incident of the three desperadoes on the *Walter Scott*. Ironically, the fake royalty not only made no profit, but are out $400. When the King and the Duke turn to their whiskey, a drunken reconciliation is patched up.

Chapter XXXI contains the climax of the entire book insofar as Huck's moral dilemma is concerned. The King and the Duke, having hit a protracted spell of bad luck, sell Jim for $40 and are busy setting up a new performance of the "Royal Nonesuch" in Pikesville when Huck learns what they have done. His whole training and background prompt him to write Miss Watson, confess that he has aided her slave to escape, and make himself right with God. But then there floods over him the tender recollection of the idyllic experiences he shared with Jim floating down the river, and he realizes that in the long run Jim's goodness, his naive but firm affection, his love for his family, and his willingness to sacrifice sleep and safety for Huck make him essentially a better man than Huck. Pestered and bewildered by the moral contradictions involved, Huck makes the naturally good decision; he renounces the church teachings and the social code of his Missouri upbringing, and courageously adheres to the moral truth of the heart. Looking at the letter he has written to Miss Watson, he meditates: "It was a close place. I took [the letter] up and held it in my hand. I was a-trembling, because I'd got to decide, forever, betwixt two things, and I knowed it. I studied a minute, sort of holding my breath, and then says to myself:

'All right, then, I'll *go* to hell'—and tore it up." This very passage has caused more than one squeamish soul to denounce this book as unfit for children. But the courage, the self-reliance, and the august dignity of the decision make this a moving and richly truthful passage.

The last eleven chapters, following this decision, have occasioned one of the most lively controversies in recent literary criticism. The body of opinion is that the ending is a weak and clownish addition, full of childish nonsense, which ought never to have been written. On the other hand, if we recall the "theme and variations" structure that we found to operate in *Tom Sawyer* and the early portions of this book, some justification can be found for the ending.

Huck goes to the plantation where he knows Jim is being held for reward; the Phelpses, who bought Jim from the King, think he belongs on a plantation south of New Orleans, since the Duke had printed up a handbill advertising Jim's escape. Miraculously enough, Huck is greeted lovingly by Aunt Sally Phelps who turns out to be Tom Sawyer's aunt. She was expecting a visit from Tom, and assumes Huck is Tom. Tom himself comes along shortly thereafter; like Jim, he thinks Huck is a ghost at first. By a hastily arranged agreement, Tom poses as Sid Sawyer. The two boys then dedicate themselves to freeing Jim.

In contrast to the Grangerford place, the Phelps farm represents "one of these little one-horse cotton plantations." In another detailed description, we learn the characteristics of a modest Southern farm where the wife does the spinning in the log house and the husband doubles as a preacher in a church he built himself. This completes the catalogue of social observations that form such a rich part of this book.

Huck's own essential goodness is illustrated again when he and Tom sneak off to town to warn the rapscallion King and Duke that word has got around about their "Royal Nonesuch" swindle; before the boys can reach them, they see the torchlight procession that rides the two tarred and feathered rogues out of town on a rail. Huck's genuine regret at seeing justice done to the two men who used him in the most unforgivable manner is one of his most endearing qualities.

Tom, the devoted romantic admirer of such prisoners as Baron Trenck, Casanova, Cellini, Henry IV, Lady Jane Grey, Guildford Dudley, Northumberland, Louis XVI, and Dumas heroes, insists that Jim's escape must be managed with all the highly involved intrigue of romantic literature, whereas it could be as simple as stealing a key and opening the door of the cabin for him. Even though he could lift the bed to release his chain from the leg, Jim must saw through the leg, eat the sawdust, cover the sawmarks, and wait. Even though Jim cannot write, he must keep a

journal on a shirt written in blood and must scratch secret mes-
sages on the backs of tin plates. Even though he is on the ground,
he must make a rope ladder. It is only with some argument that
Huck convinces Tom it is not necessary for Jim to saw off his
own leg to get rid of the chains! Undoubtedly, Clemens saw this
as raucously funny—and if one gives oneself up to this delightful
nonsense, it is highly amusing. But aesthetically, this whole ritual
reproduces in a kind of musical coda the themes of the rest of the
book. When Tom insists that Jim saw his way out of the cabin
laboriously, this repeats Huck's means of escape from Pap's cabin
at the opening of the book. When Huck must put on a girl's dress
to deliver a warning note to the Phelpses, we recall his disguise
when he visited Mrs. Loftus. When Tom insistently refuses to take
the easy way out, but must complicate the escape with gallant
flourishes, we recall that the two desperadoes could have escaped
from the *Walter Scott* if they had not gone back for more loot,
and that the King and the Duke could have escaped with the
$6,000 if they had not lingered to dispose of the Wilks house and
the slaves. In each case, Jim's advice of "better let blame' well
alone" was disregarded, to the grief of the greedy ones. We also
remember that the two *Walter Scott* desperadoes deserted their
comrade, just as Huck and the Duke deserted the King on the
third night of the "Royal Nonesuch," and just as Huck deserted the
King and the Duke at the cemetery—in the same way, Huck and
Tom are separated when they flee the Phelps plantation. Lastly,
the insistence that Jim share his cabin with rats, spiders, and rat-
tlesnakes recalls the rattlesnake incident on Jackson's Island.

The ending is complicated by melodramatic flourishes, including a visit from Aunt Polly, and the revelation that Jim has been
free all along, since Miss Watson repented and released him in
her will. Huck learns from Jim that the body they saw in the
floating house was that of his father. Thus the boy who was
thought to be dead throughout the book is alive, whereas the father who was thought to be alive is dead. The book closes on
Huck's vow "But I reckon I got to light out for the territory
ahead of the rest, because Aunt Sally she's going to adopt me and
sivilize me, and I can't stand it. I been there before."

We can easily understand why Huck hates civilization. His trip
down the river has shown him filth, brutality, hatred, violence,
and hypocrisy. At the most harmless level, he saw river-town loafers drench stray dogs with turpentine and set fire to them for
amusement; at the worst, he saw tarring and feathering, lynch

mobs, the cold-blooded murder of Boggs, and the wholesale slaughter of the Grangerford-Shepherdson feud. All this was pervaded by the chicanery of the King and the Duke. The critic Philip Young has counted thirteen corpses in the book.

To be sure, the rarer glimpses of goodness and gentleness shine forth the more brightly for this context. Jim's affectionate comradeship and Huck's decision to stand by Jim affirm man's brotherhood. The sweetness and courage of Mary Jane Wilks would be rare qualities even in the calmer society of our day. And the warm love and care given the boys by Aunt Sally Phelps is an enduring symbol of motherhood.

Huckleberry Finn is valuable as informal social history; taken along with selected chapters of *Life on the Mississippi*, it is a compendium of dress, interior decoration, manners, social conventions, and economic realities of the ante-bellum river culture. Whether the scientific linguist gives any support to Clemens' own claim about the accuracy of the dialects, this volume is inexhaustible in its verbal delight. We have Pap's illiterate and profane fulminations, the pseudo-literary pretensions of the Duke, Mrs. Loftus' housewifely locutions, Jim's Negro dialect, Colonel Sherburn's polished eloquence, and the incomparable gabble of old Mrs. Hotchkiss at the Phelpses. Above all, we have Huck's own vulgar but richly beautiful lingo, which carries the narration along as smoothly and majestically as the river itself. When he sees Aunt Polly unexpectedly standing in the doorway at the end, there is no conceivable improvement on his exclamation: "If she warn't standing right there, just inside the door, looking as sweet and contented as an angel half full of pie, I wish I may never!"

The highest accolade, however, must be reserved for the complexity of moral awareness on the part of this growing boy. By his many anguished decisions in which he is torn between the conflicting codes of social and religious conventions and the inherent truth that wells up from within, this essentially primitive and pragmatic child reduplicates the struggle of each one of us in a world that was not expressly founded for our own comfort.

Tom Sawyer Abroad is in many ways a tired book; conceived as a circumnavigation of the world in a balloon, it is cut off arbitrarily when the boys reach the Middle East. A. B. Paine says that Clemens began a book on this subject in 1868, but abandoned it when he learned that Jules Verne's *Five Weeks in a Balloon* accidentally paralleled his work; when Clemens took up the subject again, there is a distinct possibility that he was influenced by material from the Verne novel.

The bumptious Tom attempts to persuade Huck and Jim to go on a crusade, but, failing this, he takes them to St. Louis where they become the captives of a mad balloonist who whisks them across the Atlantic. After they lose the scientist in a storm, they find themselves over the Sahara, where they encounter adventures involving lions, caravans, and marauding bedouins. We catch a whiff of *The Gilded Age* in their plan to make a fortune selling little vials of Sahara sand as souvenirs. The bulk of the book consists of heated arguments in which Tom shows superior information and intelligence, but Huck and Jim repeatedly defeat him by their naive peasant practicality. They assume that all countries will be the same color as represented on the map, and they refuse to accept changes in time as they travel. They continue to quibble over interpretations of tales from *Arabian Nights,* the prowess of fleas, the reality of mirages, and whether the Sahara is waste material left over from the creation of the world. The critics who praise this volume are entranced by the "epistemological" humor, since most of the extended arguments concern degrees of certainty in human knowledge.

After sojourns at an oasis, the pyramids, and Mount Sinai, Tom breaks his corncob and sends Jim and the Arab guide back to Missouri for another. Aunt Polly catches Jim and orders the boys home immediately. Although the story is told in the first person by Huck, it lacks the verbal magic of *Huckleberry Finn.*

❧ ❧

We have already noted Clemens' fascination with the ratiocinative detective yarn; in *Tom Sawyer, Detective,* he follows the pattern of *Pudd'nhead Wilson,* revealing the true situation only during an exciting trial scene at the end.

By now, Jim has been eliminated from the trio. Tom and Huck are sent back to the Phelps plantation to provide cheerful company for Uncle Silas who has become cross and disagreeable. Benny, a Phelps daughter, was finally denied in marriage to Brace Dunlap, a rich neighboring farmer. He is now trying to ruin Uncle Silas in revenge. Part of his plan is to work through his worthless brother, Jubiter, a laborer at the Phelpses.

On the steamboat headed for Arkansas, Huck and Tom meet Jake Dunlap, the black sheep twin of Jubiter who has been thought dead for many years. Jake tells them his harrowing history, which bears some resemblance to Chaucer's "Pardoner's Tale." Jake and two accomplices stole two immense diamonds from a St. Louis jeweler, but each suspected the other of wanting to go off with the swag, so that none of them could sleep easy. By accident Jake learned that one of his companions, Bud Dixon, had hidden the diamonds in his boot heels; Jake stole the boots and fled to this very steamboat. The two companions are tracking him down, but he hopes to hide out at Brace's farm. On a stormy night he leaves the steamboat, with an agreement to meet Huck and Tom at a sycamore clump behind Uncle Silas' tobacco field, once they have ascertained the route is clear. When he leaves, however, Bud Dixon and the other accomplice, Hal Clayton, track him.

After a train of incredibly complex developments, Tom discovers a buried body which is assumed to be that of Jubiter, murdered by Uncle Silas.

At the trial, the lawyer for the "prostitution" makes the jury fairly weep for the "diseased" (this is a fair sample of the punning humor of Huck's style) and the naturally absent-minded, distracted Uncle Silas is led to confess. All the while, Tom, who is representing Uncle Silas, is lost in contemplation. Suddenly he jumps up with the solution to the murder, drawing out his explanation at great length in order to milk the crowd for the greatest effect. He explains that Brace Dunlap had planned to have Uncle Silas strike Jubiter, and then for Jubiter to flee the area, leading the neighbors to assume a murder had occurred. But when Brace and Jubiter got to the sycamore clump, they found the body of Jake, recently murdered by Bud Dixon and Hal Clayton, who were scared off by two passers-by. Then Jubiter put on Jake's disguise, and Brace returned later that night, put on a work smock of Uncle Silas', and buried the body of Jake by moonlight, observed by paid witnesses.

Tom works up to a gorgeous climax in which he removes the heels from Jubiter's boots to reveal the two stolen diamonds. The story is highly improbable and melodramatic, even though Clemens maintains in a note that the plot, taken from Swedish sources, is essentially true.

Provision is made for a ghost in familiar Clemens style, in order to incorporate typical "supernatural" humor, and the exaltation of Tom at the end of the story parallels the treatment of Kathy in "A Horse's Tale." Here the apotheosis of the clever youngster, and the implicit admiration for the bumptious adolescent, is complete when the judge declares " 'Not two in a million could 'a' done it. You are a very remarkable boy.' "

◆◎ ◎◆

As in many of the other divisions of his work, we find in Clemens' boy-literature a mixture of some of the best writing America has ever produced—and some of the worst. It is the contrast between the two extremes that perplexes the reader. The most likely explanation is that Clemens worked entirely unconsciously, neither wanting, nor maybe even knowing of, the kind of surgically rational exactitude with which an author like Flaubert would worry for days over the choice of one word. As Bernard DeVoto has remarked:

> He wrote on impulse, and when the impulse was in circuit with the deeper levels of his phantasy things went well, but when the circuit was broken he could only improvise. Improvisation was responsible for the worst and commonest blemishes in his books—and, because he could not long sustain it, for the breaking-off of many manuscripts. He had little ability to impose structure on his material; he could not think and feel it through to its own implicit form. He got 'ideas' for books, stories, or sketches and jotted them down in his notebooks where they survive by the hundred, promising or feeble but almost always undeveloped. He caught fire easily and when an 'idea' inflamed him, he attacked it with verve and enthusiasm, trusting to luck, providence, or his demon to make it good.[1]

Whether it is luck, providence, or his demon, the circuits were connected for most of *Huckleberry Finn,* and they were connected to the "deeper levels of his phantasy" simply because he cared so little, on the more superficial conscious level, for this book.

The book is as roguish and sassy as its protagonist, and it has been treated as if it were a tramp too. Hardly a year has passed when it was not banned by some library or attacked by some reformer. This began very shortly after its publication and continued throughout Clemens' life, and into our own day. To be sure, the race issue was not the same in Clemens' day as in ours, and it is partly this accident of history that has made the book topical. But the panoramic sweep of social observation, the tender love of nature, the gusty dash of human action, and the mature complexity of moral choice revealed in the book have justified it as a volume that sells nearly as steadily as the Bible.

[1] *Mark Twain at Work* (Cambridge, Massachusetts, 1942), p. 52.

8

~§ OTHER WRITINGS

C LEMENS' miscellaneous writings include a hodge-podge of material, some extremely dull and some of the highest quality.
The most representative tones can be seen in his predominantly
polemic pieces on literature (Harriet Shelley, Shakespeare, James
Fenimore Cooper), the American and the Jewish character, and
religion (Biblical parody, the book on Christian Science, the controversy with the missionaries). Lastly, the group of essays and
stories with a predominantly philosophical and moral cast includes
some pieces, notably "The Man That Corrupted Hadleyburg" and
The Mysterious Stranger, that rank high in the Clemens canon.

The polemic pieces are interesting largely as documents of obsession; if any doubts are ever to be entertained about the complete soundness of Clemens' adjustment to reality, it is here that
they would occur. He obviously never outgrew the habits of mind
engendered by frontier journalism, where the acuteness of controversy between rival newspapers reached a height of frenzy in
which the most fantastic sophistries were justified, provided they
helped boost circulation. He gives us his own tongue-in-cheek version of his apprenticeship in "Journalism in Tennessee"; the first
is a paragraph he wrote as a fledgling reporter for the *"Morning
Glory and Johnson County War-Whoop,"* and the second is his editor's revised version:

It is pleasant to note that the city of Blathersville is endeavoring
to contract with some New York gentlemen to pave its well-nigh

impassable streets with the Nicholson pavement. The *Daily Hurrah* urges the measure with ability, and seems confident of ultimate success.

Blathersville wants a Nicholson pavement—it wants a jail and a poorhouse more. The idea of a pavement in a one-horse town composed of two gin-mills, a blacksmith shop, and that mustard-plaster of a newspaper, the *Daily Hurrah!* The crawling insect, Buckner, who edits the *Hurrah,* is braying about his business with his customary imbecility, and imagining that he is talking sense.

In other words, his strength as a polemic writer lies more in rhetoric than in logic; it does not matter how an idea is arrived at, but the defense of the idea must be truculent, brilliant, and biting. Clemens described this method very succinctly in the words of the Old Man in *What Is Man?:*

'. . . there are none but temporary Truth-Seekers; . . . a permanent one is a human impossibility; . . . as soon as the Seeker finds what he is thoroughly convinced is the Truth, he seeks no further, but gives the rest of his days to hunting junk to patch it and caulk it and prop it with, and make it weather-proof and keep it from caving in on him.'

Although some form of scholarship might help him in finding the junk to patch up the ideas, he seldom looks farther than the book which originally fired his imagination, and which he is bent on attacking or defending. He delimits a complex field to a few, simple, emotionally conceived value judgments, and then he marshals all the detailed evidence he can find. In questions where no evidence is available, he builds up an elaborate deductive scaffolding on one or two rigidly arbitrary definitions. The whole argument seldom follows a consecutive development; the longer the piece, the more chaotic. In cases such as the Christian Science book, where he returned to the same subject repeatedly over a period of years, he is likely to fight the same battles in chapter after chapter, apparently backtracking because he has thought of slightly new emphases he wants to put on the material without going to the trouble of wholesale revision.

In our days of decorously ethical professional journalism, however, Clemens' boiling rages and vituperative phrases come as a welcome release. For anyone who enjoys watching others become angry, these essays present a gaudy, sputtering spectacle.

Clemens' tenderness for feminine purity, which led him to write *Joan of Arc*, combined with his love of an old-fashioned boiling rage to produce "In Defense of Harriet Shelley." It is a searing attack on Edward Dowden's biography of the poet which Clemens feels blackened Shelley's first wife's good name. Again, as in numerous similar pieces, the reader asks "What is Hecuba to him or he to Hecuba that he should weep for her?" The amount of anger and indignation displayed is in shocking contrast to the relative unimportance of the issue. We can only assume that where the moral purity of an ideally Victorian type of woman is besmirched, Clemens simply lost all sense of proportion. Shelley's abandonment of Harriet and her subsequent suicide are treated as causally connected events of criminal significance—which may be true; elsewhere in the same article, however, Clemens contradicts himself by giving high praise to all the rest of Shelley's character and achievement.

It is the same case with Shakespeare. In apprentice pilot days, Clemens worked with an ardent admirer of Shakespeare who was also an indefatigable debater. Clemens says he took up the position that Bacon was the author of the plays simply to give his friend something to argue about. In "Is Shakespeare Dead?" Clemens presents no evidence of personal scholarship, and relies on George G. Greenwood's *The Shakespeare Problem Restated* almost entirely. His argument is repetitive, sporadic, and totally without direction. It is full of overblown, bombastic pseudo-eloquence, an exaggerated pitch of a traveling salesman. The whole structure rests on the one foundation stone of Shakespeare's knowledge of the law, which Clemens finds far too expert to be the plausible expression of an unknown country-bumpkin actor.

"Fenimore Cooper's Literary Offenses" is the closest approach to purely literary criticism, since the Shelley and Shakespeare pieces are biographical. Or perhaps one should call it "literary bombardment"—Clemens vigorously attacks this romantic novelist of the frontier for eighteen documented offenses including physically improbable or impossible incidents, dialogue, style, and kindred questions. Offense number three is a fair sample:

> The rules governing literary art require that the personages in a tale shall be alive, except in the case of corpses, and that always the reader shall be able to tell the corpses from the others. But this detail has often been overlooked in the Deerslayer tale.

❧ ☙

In suppressed portions of *Life on the Mississippi,* Clemens most wholeheartedly supported the findings of early European travelers who censured American manners; but when a contemporary Frenchman, Paul Bourget, undertook in *Outre Mer* to analyze the American character, Clemens' dander was up, especially since the morals of women bulked large in the discussion. Although "What Paul Bourget Thinks of Us" is ephemeral journalism, it is a neat example of a classic line of attack, in that it first undermines Bourget's qualifications and then points out the difficulty of the task he attempted; after this, Clemens is ready for refutation of specific arguments. It is a better controlled piece than many of the others, but in a subsequent reply, "A Little Note to M. Paul Bourget," he loses the advantage by indulging in extravagantly arch irony. The most interesting sidelight of the former article is Clemens' defense of the native (and preferably the regional) novelist as the only true reflector of national character. This idea may have been pushed solely for argumentative strategy, since this is the only time he makes a point that would otherwise be his own strongest defense as a writer. Certainly the world has accepted *Huckleberry Finn* on this assumption. For the rest, Clemens spends much of his ammunition in maintaining the universality of human character.

"Concerning the Jews" is a reply to a letter written about an earlier report, "Stirring Times in Austria." On the one hand, Clemens paints himself as an unprejudiced person (with one unrevealed exception, which one suspects is Frenchmen). He maintains that Jews are on the whole benevolent, peaceful, and admirably decent citizens. But on the other hand, he sees them as a group that have been almost miraculously endowed with business acumen ever since the days of Joseph, and it is to this unpopular talent that he attributes their long history of persecution. In passing, he makes a wryly comic remark on Zionism, which was in its infancy in his day. His major objection to Jews is their failure to use their franchise and organize into politically effective national groups.

❦ ❧

We saw in Chapter I that Clemens did not consider the Bible to be divinely inspired. When we also take into account that the burlesque of Shakespeare and other classics was a stock in trade of the early journalistic milieu in which he learned to hold his pen, it is hardly surprising to find him whiling away many an hour, throughout his entire career, at humorous diaries of Biblical figures. Mercifully, little of this material has reached print. The diary of Shem, which was conceived as a grandiose and hilarious project, took its place with many another abortive effort. The diaries of Adam and of Eve have been published in short extracts that show a wide variety of aims. Adam is portrayed, in typical domestic comedy, as the lone male who is pestered and harried by the unwelcome attentions of the busybody female; the arrival of Cain and Abel is a perplexing development which Adam views suspiciously as another of Eve's inexplicable tricks. A mourning postscript Clemens added after Olivia's death gives a note of personal sentimentality that contradicts the baffled irritation that Adam felt in the rest of the diary. It also suggests that both diaries, as we shall see in a moment, were conceived as veiled presentations of the Clemenses' domestic life.

The diary of Eve is more serious, though genial, in conception, presenting the busybody tendencies of the eternal female in a light that makes her look more like the first scientist than the first housewife. Her love of natural beauty leads her to experimentation with the laws of gravity, astronomy, and biology. The account finally settles into a paean of passionate devotion to the lackadaisical and uninterested male. One senses here that Clemens is in a typically guilty mood about his own shortcomings as a husband, and means Eve's blind devotion to be a sort of exaltation of Olivia's love for an unworthy spouse. Thus both diaries taken together should perhaps be read along with the "McWilliams" stories as a unit; this would show Clemens to be an accomplished humorist in the delicate and mild area of domestic ironies.

While it is not exactly Biblical parody, "Captain Stormfield's Visit to Heaven" is a satirical attempt to destroy traditional beliefs about the nature of heaven. On his trip from California to New York, just before he set sail for Europe the first time, he was deeply impressed by the character of Captain Ned Wakeman, who formed the basis for Captain Stormfield as well as for several others of Clemens' seafaring characters. Although it was begun as early as 1868, this was one of the works his wife forbade him to publish, but like *What Is Man?* (which he published privately in 1906) this work was published after her death, in 1907, in an extract.

This is a work of high quality, strongly conceived and executed; it stands, along with "To a Person Sitting in Darkness," as a satire that can be compared very directly with the best of Jona-

Samuel L. Clemens   *The Bettmann Archive*

than Swift. The approach is permeated with the two interests we noted toward the end of Chapter I—geology and astronomy. Fascinated by the discrepancy between our own provincial view of the universe and its staggering immensity, both in space and in time, Clemens devotes himself to gleefully destroying glib Sunday School assumptions about the Promised Land.

Captain Stormfield travels at about the rate of a million miles a second, and yet it takes him thirty years to get to heaven; once there, he finds it is an incalculably immense area which reduplicates the area of the universe, but on a greatly expanded scale, obviously in order to accommodate all the dead souls throughout time. St. Peter is not at the gate, and we have no indication of who gets in and who does not—in fact, they seem rather haphazard about the matter up there. Newly arrived souls are given wings, harps, halos, and palm branches, but they tire of sitting on a cloud and singing badly within a day or so, and simply drop the accouterments by the wayside. They return, by choice, to some kind of constructive activity such as they performed on earth, and usually they also choose the age of optimum intelligence and spiritual powers of which they are capable. They ordinarily prefer to be in the area of heaven which corresponds to the area they inhabited on earth, although this makes it difficult for Americans, because European stock has occupied the area such a short time that the random white finds himself immersed in a largely Indian culture. In fact, visiting angels from other areas find so few whites in this part of heaven that they assume them to be lepers.

Another curiously upsetting fact is that heaven is a thoroughly aristocratic state. Clemens apparently chose this plan as another means of disconcerting the democratic assumption of the pious that they will commune with the prophets and patriarchs and will immediately be able to embrace Abraham and weep on his shoulder. Sandy, who becomes Captain Stormfield's informant, points out that if this were permitted, poor Abraham would be standing there all day long for centuries, constantly dripping wet! The angels consider themselves very lucky to get the slightest glimpse of an archangel once in thousands of years. But there is a rather democratic corollary in heaven to balance out this hierarchy; that is that the justice is perfect, and each man is permitted to do the job he most secretly wanted to do on earth, but which conditions may have prevented his doing. Also, all his deepest potentialities are realized. For example, a Tennessee tailor, Edward J. Billings, wrote sublime poetry, but was ignored by his neighbors; in heaven, Homer and Shakespeare do him obeisance.

The major ironic effect, as in the case of the quickly discarded wings, is that each soul is given complete freedom to choose as he will, but he usually finds that his wishes were vain, and heaven in the long run turns out to be exactly like life on earth, with the exception that the heavenly counterpart of our world—to say nothing of our nation—is a punily insignificant border territory in the universe which is only visited by those who have a taste for quaint curios, much like the modern tourist who goes to Monaco or Luxembourg.

The complete absence of the spiritual in the diaries and the visit to heaven does not mean that Clemens was insensitive in this regard; he was interested in psychic phenomena and faith cures from his early days as a journalist, and there were spiritualists in his social circle in Hartford. While his attitude is generally skeptical—with an admixture of admiration here and there—he was particularly hospitable to ideas of mental telegraphy, on which he wrote two opinionated articles. Olivia had been raised from an invalid's bed as a girl by a traveling miracle-worker. Also, he and Olivia took their daughter Jean to a Swedish faith-healer while in Europe. His daughter Clara, who published a book on the subject in 1956, is an ardent Christian Scientist.

Although he opens *Christian Science* with violent humor about faith cures, he is not on the whole hostile to the idea of curing illness in this way, and distinctly praises the placidity and calmness of mind that seem to result from an acceptance of Christian Science tenets. On the other hand, he is belligerently hostile on other issues. In fierce and repeated attacks, he belabors what he sees as Mrs. Eddy's greed for worship and for absolute power. He expends elaborate analysis on her business acumen, largely in the field of publishing, where Clemens considers himself a past expert. And lastly, he hotly maintains, on purely internal stylistic evidence, that she did not write her textbook, *Science and Health with Key to the Scriptures*. His book is a carelessly assembled hodge-podge of magazine articles padded out with filler; it has no organization or consecutive logic. Early portions were written abroad, where Clemens lacked adequate reference material, and the footnotes are a welter of subsequent retractions of earlier rash assumptions.

One wonders why he wasted so much of his time on this issue.

For one thing, impossible as it may seem, he apparently feared that the political organization and the psychological appeal of Christian Science would be more potentially dangerous to American democracy than any dark machinations of the Vatican; he speaks, for example, of entire United States Congresses of the future which will be dominated by Christian Scientists. Also, his initial articles inspired rebuttals and responses, which obviously whetted his appetite for further controversy. For the rest, his attacks on Mrs. Eddy's character and prose style are simply convenient outlets for pet peeves, like monarchism, poor English, the worship of images, and the like.

"To a Person Sitting in Darkness," is on a subject worthy of Clemens' pyrotechnic rage. In an address to the benighted pagans, he explains in a shifting and sinuous kind of irony the workings of colonial rapacity. To be sure, the opening seems a bit uncertain in direction, with its citation of prostitution, corruption, and sin in an American city, and with its sudden shift to the exorbitant reparations collected by the Reverend Ament, an American missionary, after the Boxer Rebellion. The reader makes the connection between the evil state of affairs at home and the materialistic greed of the supposedly Christian field workers in China. But then Clemens is off again on a comparison between the hypocrisy of England's position in the Boer War and analagous French and German exploitation of colonial areas. This is followed by a brilliantly corrosive invective in his address to the Filipinos about how the American colonial policy in Cuba was reversed in the Philippines at the expense of wholesale slaughter. Although the ironic pose is less consistently maintained, this piece easily takes its place beside Swift's "A Modest Proposal" for intensity of feeling and the pressure of moral outrage.

Although the remarks on the missionary appear simply to have been incidental to the indictment of imperialism, journalists and clergymen attacked Clemens vigorously for his treatment of the Reverend Ament. The particular issue was that he maintained Ament collected reparations for slaughter and damage thirteen times larger than the original value; this turned out to be an error in transmitting the cable, and the missionary collected only one third more than the original value. After an exasperatingly detailed introduction, Clemens finishes his answer "To My Missionary Critics" with a scathing denunciation of moral relativism. Ament justified the collection of this extra swag by saying it was a Chinese custom, and Clemens replied that Ament had revised the Ten Commandments thus: *"Thou shalt not steal*—except when it is the custom in the country."

It was the same spirit that inspired his famous New Year's greeting from the Nineteenth Century to the Twentieth, published in the New York *Herald* on December 30, 1900:

> I bring you the stately matron named Christendom, returning bedraggled, besmirched and dishonored from pirate-raids in Kiao-Chou, Manchuria, South Africa & the Philippines, with her soul full of meanness, her pocket full of boodle and her mouth full of pious hypocrisies. Give her soap and a towel, but hide the looking-glass.

It is a relatively easy transition from the polemical writings to the "philosophical" ones, since *What Is Man?*—the major document in the category of thoughtful writing—is largely argumentative in form and intent. It also resembles the polemical writings in that it represents an obsessive preoccupation with one particular cluster of ideas.

The plan for this book haunted him for a long time, and although he wrote it out earlier, he was prevented from publishing it by his wife's irrevocable disapproval. In 1883 he read to a club in Hartford "What Is Happiness?" a document that was the basis for several chapters of *What Is Man?* In the strong reaction that greeted the reading of this paper, Clemens felt himself justified since he interpreted the outraged feelings of the audience as typical of those of any hypocrite when presented with fundamental truth.

The philosophy involved is quite simple. To "What Is Happiness?" he answers: exclusive satisfaction of one's own temperamental and spiritual needs; and to *What Is Man?* he answers: an exteriorly determined machine, with no originality of idea and no freedom of will.

The form for these ideas is a dialogue between an Old Man who presents the theory with all of Clemens' bumptiousness and irascible superiority, and a Young Man who holds to the ordinary Christian assumptions about man and morals. The progress of the dialogue is just as chaotically managed as in the other polemic pieces; if there is any virtue in the organization, it is that each section, at least, is concentrated on one topic, but the progression from section to section is haphazard.

He maintains that man is a machine, totally without command

over itself; there is the *donnée* of a temperament and of certain predispositions, but after granting that, he insists that training (meaning the incessant bombardment of exterior influences, including all the unconscious assimilation of environment) does the rest. In the moral sphere, we act out of a need for self-satisfaction; no matter what kind of sacrifices we make—and he adduces numberless anecdotal examples—it is always to soothe our own consciences. He is not disturbed by the fact that different consciences desire different things, because it is the same mechanism at work. One always satisfies No. 1, and whatever happens to Nos. 2, 3, 4, and the rest is irrelevant to No. 1. But then, curiously enough, this issues in an Admonition which the Old Man gives the Young:

'Diligently train your ideals *upward* and *still upward* toward a summit where you will find your chiefest pleasure in conduct which, while contenting you, will be sure to confer benefits upon your neighbor and the community.'

But the reader with a few more dialectical resources than the poor Young Man in the dialogue may ask "Why bother with all this *upward* business? Does a machine recognize such a moral dimension—particularly a self-satisfying machine?" Clemens has already proven that acting for social approval is not valid, since the innate temperaments of some persons do not crave that kind of satisfaction. He does speak in the dialogue as if there were a God who created these machines, but he never settles the obviously glaring problem of a machine's caring about its creator enough to want to have its ideals trained *"upward."* Nor does he say enough about God for us to know whether He even desires this upward movement.

He carries on with three well-worn dichotomies: man-animal, mind-body, and free will-determinism. He disposes of the first by maintaining that instinct is simply petrified thought, and that animals are capable of a rudimentary thought, the only difference being that man has a more refined mechanism with which to perform the act. On the whole, he implies, animals are superior to men in the moral sphere because they never knowingly do evil. This is an issue we shall re-encounter in *The Mysterious Stranger*. The mind-body dichotomy he leaves as confused as when he initially stated it. As for the third problem he rejects free will, but retains mental "free choice" which is simply a rational judgment of good and evil, unenforceable because the temperament blindly wills what it wishes with no interference from the mind.

Although we are admittedly looking back at Clemens from a vantage point that makes many of his ideas look simple and trite, it is not just due to progress since his day; the ideas were trite philosophically and psychologically even in his day. Even a rudimentary acquaintance with Plato or Aristotle or Augustine or Descartes would have rendered his intellectual bombs innocuous. This is not to say that his ideas lack interest or value in themselves, because they do deal, particularly in the psychological sphere, with fundamental issues. Clemens simply lacks the refinement and polish of a fundamental liberal education which is the *sine qua non* for speculation of the sort he wanted to make later in his life. With this prerequisite, he would have seen that these problems had been exhaustively investigated by better minds than his and that such private speculations are not the scandalous horrors his Young Man takes them to be, but simply an uneducated layman's mental meanderings.

As for Clemens' own attitude toward holding such a philosophy, he is convinced it is rock-hard fact; promulgating it can do no harm, even though the Young Man toward the end warns him it could cause immense damage. If man is simply a machine formed by exterior influences, then this dialogue would just become one more exterior influence within a social context that contains many others. At a deeper level, Clemens is obviously emotionally satisfied by holding a kind of curmudgeon's view of things without being especially bitter about it. As he wrote to Howells:

> What I have been wanting was a chance to write a book without reserves—a book which should take account of no one's feelings, no one's prejudices, opinions, beliefs, hopes, illusions, delusions; a book which should say my say, right out of my heart, in the plainest language & without a limitation of any sort. I judged that that would be an unimaginable luxury, heaven on earth. There was no condition but one under which the writing of such a book could be possible; only one—the consciousness that it would not see print.
>
> It is under way, now, & it *is* a luxury! an intellectual drunk. . . .
>
> I hope it will take me a year or two to write it, & that it will turn out to be the right vessel to contain all the ordure I am planning to dump into it.[1]

"The Man That Corrupted Hadleyburg" illustrates many of these assumptions in the realm of morality. This corrupter is a

---

[1] Henry Nash Smith and William M. Gibson, eds., *Mark Twain–Howells Letters* (Cambridge, Massachusetts, The Belknap Press of Harvard University Press, 1960), pp. 698–9.

mysterious stranger who leaves a sack containing about $40,000 in gold with the Richardses; accompanying it is a note indicating that the stranger was helped by a native of Hadleyburg, which is noted far and wide for its uprightness and honesty. When the native helped the stranger, he gave the hungry man $20.00 (so the note says) along with some words of advice; the stranger made the fortune in the sack by gambling, but then the advice sank home, and he reformed himself. He now has left the words of advice in a sealed envelope to be opened in the church in exactly one month by the Rev. Mr. Burgess, and on that occasion, the benefactor can claim the gold by turning in an envelope with the words of advice written out.

The Richardses immediately assume that the only man in town who would help a stranger would be the now deceased Mr. Goodson, the others being too stingy, narrow, and proud of their honesty to perform a good deed. Indeed, many years before, Richards saw an illustration of Goodson's benevolence. When the minister, Burgess, was in disgrace, Richards knew that the minister was really innocent. Since Richards could not afford to face the social disapproval of revealing this, Mr. Goodson bore the brunt of the town disapproval while in the meantime Richards secretly warned the minister to leave the town for safety.

During the month before the sack is opened, the Associated Press gives the honest town of Hadleyburg nation-wide publicity, while each of the nineteen leading citizens quietly plans what he will do with the $40,000. Each of them has received a letter from a stranger confirming that it was Goodson who did the good deed, but that when Goodson died, he said he wished he could give a fortune to this particular person; the correspondent then reveals that the words spoken by Goodson to the stranger were "You are far from being a bad man: Go, and reform." Each, of course, secretly slips the Reverend Burgess an envelope containing these words.

On the Friday evening on which the envelopes are opened, eighteen of the citizens are revealed to have tried to gain the money dishonestly, and the reputation of the town is now lost for good. As an added fillip, the note in the sack contains the same words the eighteen citizens gave, but adds "Go, and reform—or, mark my words—some day, for your sins, you will die and go to hell or Hadleyburg—TRY AND MAKE IT THE FORMER."

The minister, wishing to repay Richards for his earlier kindness, does not reveal that the latter, too, submitted an envelope, and the town, assuming Richards is honest, wishes to reward him. A stranger (Mr. Stephenson, who arranged the whole hoax) reveals that the coins are simply gilded lead, and proposes an auction of the coins, onto which the names of the eighteen will be stamped, the proceeds of the auction to go to Mr. Richards. Pinkerton, the banker, and Harkness, a patent medicine magnate, are involved in a political contest, and cannot afford to have their names so disgraced. Harkness buys up the sack of coins from Stephenson for $40,000, which he passes on to the Richardses at Stephenson's request. The couple are torn by pangs of conscience, which are only augmented when the Reverend Burgess tells them he suppressed their note because Richards had shown him a kindness (which we remember was no kindness at all, but an effort to save Richards' own neck). The old couple become ill, and in their final delirium, tear up the reward checks and reveal their own guilt in the situation.

This is one of Clemens' major indictments of what he called "the damned human race." It illustrates the assumptions of *What Is Man?* in that every leading citizen of the town follows his own self-interest, knowing all along what would be the right thing to do, but doing the wrong. Rational "free choice" indicated to them that they had no right to the money, but their wills were powerless to renounce the wealth. On the other hand, the Richardses have managed to conceal their duplicity from the entire town, and could easily escape with the money, but their consciences do them in. Here Clemens underscores his continuing hatred for what he considers the most useless aspect of the human psyche.

Although "The Man That Corrupted Hadleyburg" does not reach the heights of Clemens' best fiction, it is a superior example of "situational" fiction, in which everything depends on a heavily plotted involvement whose denouement makes a climactic philosophical point. In order for the situation to work itself out properly, depth of characterization must be sacrificed, so that the reader comes away from the tale very excited, but not as deeply moved as he would be by the richness of human observation given him in the portraits of Huck Finn, Roxana, or Colonel Sellers.

The heavy emphasis on honesty and on the corroding psychological effects of conscience must represent a profound influence in Clemens' own bringing-up, since these are major preoccupations in several of his other moral stories. "Was It Heaven? Or Hell?" also concerns itself with a problem in honesty, drawn from the Clemens family history. It centers about the problem of the family's having to lie to a sick person in order not to excite her, and thus incurring profound sin, but for essentially good motives.

Unlike *What Is Man?* and "Captain Stormfield's Visit to Heaven," *The Mysterious Stranger,* a hauntingly strange and absorbing tale of Clemens' later period, did not reach print during his life. Although the entire book as he conceived it remained unfinished, the published extract stands among Clemens' greatest productions, even if his biographer assures us that parts of the manuscript contain typically tiresome stretches.

A remote village of sixteenth-century Austria is already disturbed by the suspension of Father Peter from priestly duties because of the rumor that he told his niece, Marget, that all souls will be saved at Judgment Day. Into Eseldorf comes Satan, alias Philip Traum, an angel and nephew of the celebrated forbear of the same name. Beautiful and persuasive, Philip shows himself first to a trio of little boys, Nikolaus Bauman, the son of a judge, Seppi Wohlmeyer, the innkeeper's son, and the narrator, Theodor Fischer, whose father is town organist. Philip comes upon the boys just after they have spent a night with Felix Brandt, the oldest servingman in the local castle, who shows them ghosts and regales them with stories of the supernatural. Philip starts the boys' pipe by blowing on it, and also turns water to ice by the same means; once he has persuaded them not to run away from him, he breathes life into hundreds of little clay figures who build a miniature castle for the boys, which Philip then destroys, much to the boys' consternation. He explains that being an angel who has not tasted of the fruit of the tree, as have his Uncle Satan and humankind, he cannot know what evil is or how it differs from good. The rest of the tale is a complication of this basic situation as it works itself out in the life of the town.

Philip arranges for Father Peter to find his purse in the road, filled with enough gold coins to pay his mortgage and leave him a fortune besides; but the astrologer who originally had the priest suspended claims that Father Peter stole the money from him and has him jailed. Then Philip succors Marget and Ursula, the helpless niece and servingwoman. In the meantime, he shows Theodor a heretic being tortured to death and a French village starving because of slave-like economic exploitation. He objects to Theodor's calling such things "brutal," since the "higher" brutes are incapable of such cruelty:

'No brute ever does a cruel thing—that is the monopoly of those with the Moral Sense. When a brue inflicts pain he does it innocently; it is not wrong; for him there is no such thing as wrong. And he does not inflict pain for the pleasure of inflicting it—only man does that. Inspired by that mongrel Moral Sense of his! A sense whose function is to distinguish between right and wrong, with liberty to choose which of them he will do. Now what advantage can he get out of that? He is always choosing, and in nine cases out of ten he prefers the wrong. There shouldn't be any wrong; and without the Moral Sense there couldn't be any. And yet he is such an unreasoning creature that he is not able to perceive that the Moral Sense degrades him to the bottom layer of animated beings and is a shameful possession.'

Satan uses the occasion of a flying visit to China to indoctrinate Theodor in the deterministic mechanism by which fate is arranged; the first act of the infant determines his entire train of fate, but paradoxically, one minute's change in the course of determined events can change the entire remainder of a life. By having Nikolaus awaken one night to close the window against the rain, Satan causes him to sleep several minutes later the next morning; thus he arrives too late at the lake in which Lisa is to drown, thereby causing both to die, whereas they would have lived otherwise. He answers Theodor's horror by showing that had they lived, both children would drag along in paralysis, misery, hunger, and poverty. Satan continues this game, always interfering in order to cause a painful death or madness as a release from an even more ghastly life. He treats the two remaining boys to a quick review of human history, somewhat the reverse of that in Milton's *Paradise Lost,* in which the Christian epochs are distinguished from the earlier bloodshed and cruelty by the power and refinement of the methods of warfare.

The published portion ends with a sensational trial, much like those in *Pudd'nhead Wilson* and *Tom Sawyer, Detective,* in which young Wilhelm, Marget's beau, exonerates Father Peter after the case seemed lost, by pointing out that the date on the coins proves they could never have been the possession of the astrologer. The book concludes with Satan's revelation to Theodor that there is no afterlife, nor, indeed, any reality at all:

'It is true, that which I have revealed to you; there is no God, no universe, no human race, no earthly life, no heaven, no hell. It is all a dream—a grotesque and foolish dream. Nothing exists but you. And you are but a *thought*—a vagrant thought, a useless thought, a homeless thought, wandering forlorn among the empty eternities!'

Thus he repudiates all of creation, just as he had to Howells:

> Why *was* the human race created? Or at least why wasn't something creditable created in place of it. God had His opportunity; He could have made a reputation. But no, He must commit this grotesque folly—a lark which must have cost him a regret or·two when He came to think it over & observe effects.[2]

As for the causes of Clemens' whole latter-day attitude, as represented by *What Is Man?*, "The Man That Corrupted Hadleyburg," and *The Mysterious Stranger*, it is easy to see that Clemens needed release from the oppressive and crippling guilt feelings that characterized his personality from its earliest days; and he needed an antidote to the senselessly unjust Sunday School doctrines of his childhood, which always stand behind his mature philosophical pronouncements. This solution is an organic outgrowth of these factors. Some readers and critics with a flair for drama characterize these doctrines as sudden and late developments in his thought, induced by grief at the deaths of his wife and daughters, old age, bankruptcy, and the like; but we have seen that he encountered and embraced the deterministic ideas of McFarlane even before his steamboat days. The suppression of some of these pieces, and the posthumous publication of *The Mysterious Stranger* add their touch of drama, too, to what would otherwise appear to be what it is—the ordinary and logical consequence of Sam Clemens' development.

[2] *Mark Twain–Howells Letters,* p. 716.

SELECTED BIBLIOGRAPHY

NOTE: Works available in paperbound editions are so indicated at the conclusion of the entry.

TWAIN'S CHIEF WORKS

The Celebrated Jumping Frog of Calaveras County, and Other Sketches. New York: C. H. Webb, 1867.

The Innocents Abroad. Hartford: American Publishing Co., 1869.

Roughing It. Hartford: American Publishing Co., 1872. (Paperbound)

The Gilded Age (with Charles Dudley Warner). Hartford: American Publishing Co., 1873–4.

Mark Twain's Sketches, New and Old. Hartford: American Publishing Co., 1875.

The Adventures of Tom Sawyer. Hartford: American Publishing Co., 1876. (Paperbound)

A True Story and the Recent Carnival of Crime. Boston: J. R. Osgood, 1877.

A Tramp Abroad. Hartford: American Publishing Co., 1880.

The Prince and the Pauper. Boston: J. R. Osgood, 1882.

The Stolen White Elephant. Boston: J. R. Osgood, 1882.

Life on The Mississippi. Boston: J. R. Osgood, 1883 (first complete edition by Edward Wagenknecht, New York: Limited Editions Club, 1944). (Paperbound)

Adventures of Huckleberry Finn. New York: Charles L. Webster, 1885. (Paperbound)

A Connecticut Yankee in King Arthur's Court. New York: Charles L. Webster, 1889. (Paperbound)

The American Claimant. New York: Charles L. Webster, 1892.

The £1,000,000 Bank Note and Other New Stories. New York: Charles L. Webster, 1893.

Tom Sawyer Abroad. New York: Charles L. Webster, 1894.

The Tragedy of Pudd'nhead Wilson and the Comedy of Those Extraordinary Twins. Hartford: American Publishing Co., 1894. (Paperbound)

Personal Recollections of Joan of Arc. New York: Harper, 1896.

Tom Sawyer, Detective, and Other Stories. New York: Harper, 1896.

Following the Equator. Hartford: American Publishing Co., 1897.

How to Tell a Story and Other Essays. New York: Harper, 1897.

The Man that Corrupted Hadleyburg and Other Stories and Essays. New York: Harper, 1900.

A Double Barrelled Detective Story. New York: Harper, 1902.

A Dog's Tale. New York: Harper, 1904.

What is Man? Privately printed, 1906.

The $30,000 Bequest and Other Stories. New York: Harper, 1906.

Eve's Diary. New York: Harper, 1906.

Christian Science. New York: Harper, 1907.

A Horse's Tale. New York: Harper, 1907.

Is Shakespeare Dead? New York: Harper, 1909.

Extracts from Captain Stormfield's Visit to Heaven. New York: Harper, 1909. (A more complete edition is Dixon Wecter's *Report from Paradise,* New York: Harper, 1952.)

Works Published After Twain's Death

The Mysterious Stranger. New York: Harper, 1916.

Europe and Elsewhere. New York: Harper, 1923.

Selected Bibliography

Mark Twain's Autobiography, ed. A. B. Paine. 2 vols. New York:
   Harper, 1924.
Mark Twain in Eruption, ed. Bernard DeVoto. New York: Harper,
   1940.
The Autobiography of Mark Twain, ed. Charles Neider. New York:
   Harper, 1959.
Mark Twain and the Government, ed. Sven Peterson. Caldwell, Idaho:
   Caxton Printers, 1960.
"Ah, Sin," A Dramatic Work by Mark Twain and Bret Harte, ed.
   Frederick Anderson. San Francisco: Book Club of California, 1961.
Letters from the Earth, ed. Bernard DeVoto. New York: Harper and
   Row, 1962.

LETTERS

Mark Twain's Letters, ed. A. B. Paine. 2 vols. New York: Harper,
   1917.
Mark Twain's Letters to Will Bowen, ed. Theodore Hornberger. Austin:
   University of Texas, 1941.
Mark Twain: Business Man, ed. Samuel Charles Webster. Boston: Lit-
   tle, Brown, 1946.
The Love Letters of Mark Twain, ed. Dixon Wecter. New York:
   Harper, 1949.
Mark Twain to Mrs. Fairbanks, ed. Dixon Wecter. San Marino, Cal.:
   Huntington Library, 1949.
Twins of Genius, ed. Guy A. Cardwell. East Lansing: Michigan State
   College Press, 1953. [Correspondence with G. W. Cable.]
Mark Twain-Howells Letters, eds. Henry Nash Smith and William M.
   Gibson. 2 vols. Cambridge: Belknap Press of Harvard University
   Press, 1960. [Many separate letters appear in periodicals such as
   American Literature.]
Mark Twain's Letters to Mary, ed. Lewis Leary. New York: Columbia
   University Press, 1961.
The Pattern for Mark Twain's Roughing It: *Letters from Nevada by
   Samuel and Orion Clemens, 1861–1862,* ed. Franklin R. Rogers.
   Berkeley: University of California Press, 1961.

SPEECHES

Mark Twain's Speeches. New York: Harper, 1910 and 1923.
[Many speeches and lectures are given in various articles by Professor
   Fred W. Lorch in issues of *American Literature.*]

NOTEBOOKS

Mark Twain's Notebooks, ed. A. B. Paine. New York: Harper, 1935.

COLLECTED WORKS

The Writings of Mark Twain, ed. A. B. Paine. 37 vols. New York:
   Harper, 1923–25. [Author's National Edition. 25 vols. New York:
   Harper, 1907–18. Underwood Edition. 25 vols. New York: New-
   begin, 1901–07.]

EPHEMERAL WRITINGS COLLECTED IN BOOK FORM

The Curious Republic of Gondour and Other Whimsical Sketches. New
   York: Boni & Liveright, 1919.

Sketches of the Sixties (with Bret Harte). San Francisco: J. Howell, 1926.

The Adventures of Thomas Jefferson Snodgrass, ed. Charles Honce. Chicago: P. Covici, 1928.

Mark Twain's Letters from the Sandwich Islands, ed. G. Ezra Dane. Palo Alto: Stanford University Press, 1938.

The Washoe Giant in San Francisco, ed. Franklin Walker. San Francisco: George Fields, 1938.

Letters from Honolulu, ed. Thomas Nickerson. Honolulu: Thomas Nickerson, 1939.

Mark Twain's Travels with Mr. Brown, eds. Franklin Walker and G. Ezra Dane. New York: Knopf, 1940.

Republican Letters, ed. Cyril Clemens. Webster Groves, Mo.: International Mark Twain Society, 1941.

Mark Twain's Letters in the Muscatine Journal, ed. Edgar M. Branch. Chicago: The Mark Twain Association of America, 1942.

Washington in 1868, ed. Cyril Clemens. Webster Groves, Mo.: International Mark Twain Society, 1943.

The Letters of Quintus Curtius Snodgrass, ed. Ernest E. Leisy. Dallas: Southern Methodist University Press, 1946.

Mark Twain and Hawaii, ed. Walter Francis Frear. Chicago: Privately printed by Lakeside Press, 1947.

Mark Twain in Three Moods, ed. Dixon Wecter. San Marino, Cal.: Friends of the Huntington Library, 1948.

Mark Twain of the Enterprise, eds. Henry Nash Smith and Frederick Anderson. Berkeley and Los Angeles: University of California Press, 1957.

Mark Twain: San Francisco Virginia City Territorial Enterprise Correspondent, eds. Henry Nash Smith and Frederick Anderson. San Francisco: Book Club of California, 1957.

Traveling with the Innocents Abroad, ed. Daniel Morely McKeithan. Norman: University of Oklahoma Press, 1958.

Contributions to the Galaxy, 1868–1871, ed. Bruce McElderry. Gainesville, Florida: Scholars Facsimiles and Reprints, 1961.

Life as I Find It, ed. Charles Neider. Garden City, New York: Hanover House, 1961.

Mark Twain on the Art of Writing, ed. Martin B. Fried. Buffalo, New York: Salisbury Club, 1961. [Three essays published in the Buffalo Express, 1869–1870.]

BIBLIOGRAPHY

Standard Work

Johnson, Merle. *A Bibliography of the Works of Mark Twain,* rev. ed. New York: Harper, 1935.

Others

Asselineau, Roger. *The Literary Reputation of Mark Twain from 1910–1950.* Paris: Didier, 1954.

Benson, Ivan. "Periodical Bibliography: Bibliography of the Writings of Mark Twain in the Newspapers and Magazines of Nevada and California, 1861–1866," *Mark Twain's Western Years.* Stanford, Cal.: Stanford University Press, 1938.

Blanck, Jacob. *Bibliography of American Literature.* Vol. 2. New Haven: Yale University Press, 1957.

Branch, Edgar M. "A Chronological Bibliography of the Writings of

Samuel Clemens to June 8, 1867," *American Literature* (May, 1946).

Brashear, Minnie M. "Mark Twain's Juvenilia," *American Literature* (March, 1930).

Clark, Harry Hayden. "Mark Twain," *Eight American Authors: A Review of Research and Criticism,* ed. Floyd Stovall. New York: Modern Language Association of America, 1956.

Leary, Lewis. *Articles on American Literature, 1900–1950.* Durham: Duke University Press, 1954.

Potter, John K. *Samuel L. Clemens, First Editions and Values.* Chicago: The Black Archer Press, 1932.

Spiller, Robert E., *et al. Literary History of the United States,* Vol. III, *Bibliography.* New York: Macmillan, 1948. *Supplement,* ed. Richard M. Ludwig. New York: Macmillan, 1959.

[See also *Index to Articles on American Literature, 1951–1959.* Reference Department, University of Pennsylvania Library. Boston: G. K. Hall, 1960.]

BIOGRAPHY

Standard Works

Ferguson, DeLancey. *Mark Twain: Man and Legend.* Indianapolis: Bobbs-Merrill, 1943. [The best single volume on Twain.]

Paine, A. B. *Mark Twain: A Biography.* 3 vols. New York: Harper, 1912. [Not entirely reliable.]

Wecter, Dixon. *Sam Clemens of Hannibal,* ed. Elizabeth Wecter. Boston: Houghton Mifflin, 1952. [Contains the most exciting presentation of Clemens' childhood and adolescence.]

Others

Allen, Jerry. *The Adventures of Mark Twain.* Boston: Little, Brown, 1954.

Andrews, Kenneth R. *Nook Farm: Mark Twain's Hartford Circle.* Cambridge: Harvard University Press, 1950.

Benson, Ivan. *Mark Twain's Western Years.* Stanford, Cal.: Stanford University Press, 1938.

Branch, Edgar M. *The Literary Apprenticeship of Mark Twain.* Urbana: University of Illinois Press, 1950.

Brashear, Minnie M. *Mark Twain, Son of Missouri.* Chapel Hill: University of North Carolina Press, 1934.

Brooks, Van Wyck. *The Ordeal of Mark Twain,* rev. ed. New York: Dutton, 1933. (Paperbound)

Canby, Henry Seidel. *Turn West, Turn East.* Boston: Houghton Mifflin, 1951. [A biographical comparison with Henry James.]

Clemens, Clara. *My Father: Mark Twain.* New York: Harper, 1931.

Clemens, Will M. *Mark Twain.* San Francisco: Clemens, 1892.

DeVoto, Bernard. *Mark Twain's America.* Boston: Little, Brown, 1932.

Fatout, Paul. *Mark Twain on the Lecture Circuit.* Bloomington: Indiana University Press, 1960.

Frear, Walter Francis. *Mark Twain and Hawaii.* Chicago: Privately printed by Lakeside Press, 1947.

Gillis, William R. *Goldrush Days with Mark Twain.* New York: A. & C. Boni, 1930.

Harnsberger, Caroline Thomas. *Mark Twain: Family Man.* New York: The Citadel Press, 1960.

Henderson, Archibald. *Mark Twain.* New York: Stokes, 1911.

Howells, William Dean. *My Mark Twain.* New York: Harper, 1910.

Lawton, Mary. *A Lifetime with Mark Twain, the Memories of Katy Leary, For Thirty Years His Faithful and Devoted Servant.* New York: Harcourt, Brace, 1925.

Leacock, Stephen. *Mark Twain.* New York: Appleton, 1933.

Mack, Effie Mona. *Mark Twain in Nevada.* New York: Scribner, 1947.

Masters, Edgar Lee. *Mark Twain: A Portrait.* New York: Scribner, 1938.

Meltzer, Milton. *Mark Twain Himself: A Pictorial Biography.* New York: Thomas Y. Crowell, 1960.

Quick, Dorothy. *Enchantment, A Little Girl's Friendship with Mark Twain.* Norman: University of Oklahoma Press, 1961.

Turner, Arlin. *Mark Twain and G. W. Cable: The Record of a Literary Friendship.* East Lansing: Michigan State University Press, 1960. [Largely Cable's Letters.]

Wagenknecht, Edward. *Mark Twain, The Man and His Work,* rev. ed. Norman: University of Oklahoma Press, 1961.

Wallace, Elizabeth. *Mark Twain and the Happy Island.* Chicago: A. C. McClurg, 1913.

ANALYSIS AND CRITICISM

Separate Works

Bellamy, Gladys Carmen. *Mark Twain as a Literary Artist.* Norman: University of Oklahoma Press, 1950. [The best single volume devoted almost entirely to literary criticism.]

✓ Blair, Walter. *Mark Twain and Huck Finn.* Berkeley and Los Angeles: University of California Press, 1960.

Budd, Louis J. *Mark Twain: Social Philosopher.* Bloomington: Indiana University Press, 1962.

Covici, Pascal, Jr. *Mark Twain's Humor, The Image of a World.* Dallas, Texas: Southern Methodist University Press, 1962.

DeVoto, Bernard. *Mark Twain at Work.* Cambridge: Harvard University Press, 1942. [Also contains new manuscript material.]

Foner, Philip S. *Mark Twain: Social Critic.* New York: International Publishers, 1958.

Hemminghaus, Edgar H. *Mark Twain in Germany.* New York: Columbia University Press, 1939.

Krumplemann, John T. *Mark Twain and the German Language.* Baton Rouge: Louisiana State University Studies, No. 3, 1953.

Leary, Lewis, ed. *A Casebook on Mark Twain's Wound.* New York: Thomas Y. Crowell Company, 1962.

——. *Mark Twain.* Minneapolis: University of Minnesota Press, 1960.

✓ Long, E. Hudson. *Mark Twain Handbook.* New York: Hendricks House, 1957.

Lynn, Kenneth S. *Mark Twain and Southwestern Humor.* Boston: Little, Brown, 1960. [Both an admirable study of Twain's relation to a tradition and a fresh interpretation of his major works.]

McKeithan, Daniel M. *Court Trials in Mark Twain and Other Essays.* The Hague, Netherlands: M. Nijoff, 1958.

Marks, Barry A., ed. *Mark Twain's Huckleberry Finn.* Boston: D. C. Heath, 1959. (Paperbound)

Neider, Charles. *Mark Twain and the Russians.* New York: Hill and Wang, 1960. [A short exchange of letters between Mr. Neider and Y. Bereznitsky.]

Rogers, Franklin R. *Mark Twain's Burlesque Patterns as seen in the Novels and Narratives, 1855–1885.* Dallas: Southern Methodist University Press, 1960.

145

Selected Bibliography

Scott, Arthur L., ed. *Mark Twain, Selected Criticism*. Dallas: Southern Methodist University Press, 1955.

Smith, Henry Nash. *Mark Twain, The Development of a Writer*. Cambridge, Massachusetts: The Belknap Press of Harvard University Press, 1962.

Solomon, Roger B. *Mark Twain and the Image of History*. New Haven: Yale University Press, 1961.

Stone, Albert E., Jr. *The Innocent Eye, Childhood in Mark Twain's Imagination*. New Haven: Yale University Press, 1961.

Taylor, Coley B. *Mark Twain's Margins on Thackeray's Swift*. New York: Gotham House, 1935.

General Studies Containing Chapters on Twain

Galinsky, Hans, ed. *The Frontier in American History and Literature*. Frankfurt: Diesterweg, 1960.

Gohdes, Clarence. "Mirth for the Million," *The Literature of the American People,* ed. A. H. Quinn. New York: Appleton-Century-Crofts, 1951.

Hoffman, Daniel G. *Form and Fable in American Fiction*. New York: Oxford University Press, 1961.

Taylor, Walter F. *The Economic Novel in America*. Chapel Hill: University of North Carolina Press, 1942.

Wagenknecht, Edward. *Cavalcade of the American Novel*. New York: Holt, 1952.

Wecter, Dixon. "Mark Twain," *Literary History of the United States,* Vol. II. New York: Macmillan, 1948.

General Studies of Humor with Chapters on Twain

Blair, Walter. *Native American Humor: 1800–1900*. New York: American Book Co., 1937. (Paperbound)

———. *Horse Sense in American Humor*. Chicago: University of Chicago Press, 1942.

Tall Tales of the Southwest, ed. Franklin J. Meine. New York: Knopf, 1946.

Rourke, Constance. *American Humor*. New York: Harcourt, Brace, 1931. (Paperbound)

RECOLLECTIONS OF MARK TWAIN ANECDOTES

Clemens, Cyril. *Mark Twain, Wit and Wisdom*. New York: Stokes, 1935.

Fisher, Henry W. *Abroad with Mark Twain and Eugene Field*. New York: N. L. Brown, 1922.

Read, Opie. *Mark Twain and I*. Chicago: Reilly and Lee, 1940.

TWAIN IN HISTORICAL–PHILOSOPHICAL PERSPECTIVE

Parrington, Vernon L. "The Backwash of the Frontier—Mark Twain," *Main Currents in American Thought,* Vol. 3. New York: Harcourt, Brace, 1927–30. (Paperbound)

❦

A wealth of valuable material is contained in various journals of which one, *American Literature,* should certainly be consulted. Two journals devoted exclusively to Clemens are *The Twainian,* 1939–41 (New Series, 1942—) and the *Mark Twain Quarterly,* 1936—.

INDEX

Fictional names in Twain's works are entered in small capital letters.

147

Index

Index